OOPS!

RHINO

OOPS!

A Stupefying Survey
Of Goofs, Blunders & Botches,
Great & Small

By Paul Kirchner

GENERAL PUBLISHING GROUP
Los Angeles

Publisher: W. Quay Hays
Editor: Harold Bronson
Managing Editor: Colby Allerton
Art Director: Susan Anson
Production Director: Nadeen Torio
Color and Pre-Press Director: Gaston Moraga
Projects Manager: Trudihope Schlomowitz
Production Assistants: Tom Archibeque, Alan Peak

For information:
General Publishing Group, Inc.
2701 Ocean Park Boulevard, Suite 140
Santa Monica, CA 90405

Printed in the USA
10 9 8 7 6 5 4 3 2 1

General Publishing Group
Los Angeles

INTRODUCTION

What is history? The traditional "Great Man" theory holds that powerful individuals mold events. It was challenged by Marx's view that history is economic, an eternal class struggle. There are feminist and multicultural perspectives now as well. In this book I offer evidence that the course of human history has been determined by error as much as anything else. As voices of the past echo through the corridors of time, there is one plaintive cry that drowns out all others, a cry that encapsulates the essential nature of the human predicament, and that cry is "Oops!"

They say that oops is the one word that surgeons must never utter; the stakes for which they play are too high to acknowledge error. The same might be said for presidents, generals and billionaires; but being human, err they must. In this compendium we look at a wide selection of goofs, gaffes and screwups, whose consequences range from mere individual embarrassment to the collapse of nations. Faced with an endless supply, I have tried to bypass the tragic in favor of the comic. You decide which is which.

ACKNOWLEDGMENTS

All photos were supplied by Movie Still Archives, Harrison, Nebraska (308) 668-2302.

Invaluable assistance was provided by the Hamden Public Library, the New Haven Public Library, Magnum Photos, Dr. John Kirchner, Harold Bronson, Neil Werde, Colby Allerton and Joni Solomon.

All drawings by the author.

To Harold and Kiki

ACCIDENTS WILL HAPPEN

A worker dropped a 50¢ paint scraper into a torpedo launcher of the U.S. nuclear submarine *Swordfish* in September 1978 and jammed the loading piston. Divers spent a week attempting to free the piston at sea, without success. The *Swordfish* had to be put in drydock, and repairs ended up costing $171,000.

In the same year the Tennessee Valley Authority had to shut down a nuclear power plant for 17 days after one of a worker's galoshes fell into the atomic reactor.

In September 1980, while performing routine maintenance in a Titan II ICBM silo in Damascus, Arkansas, an air force repairman dropped a wrench socket. The socket fell into the silo and struck the missile, causing a leak in a pressurized fuel tank. The missile complex and surrounding area had to be evacuated, and a massive explosion eight hours later blew off the 740-ton silo hatch and threw the nuclear warhead 600 feet in the air. Fortunately, the warhead did not explode; as it was, one man was killed and 11 others injured in the incident.

A seven-year-old boy stranded 350 passengers and caused $750,000 worth of damage to a Boeing 747 at a stopover at Shannon International Airport in Ireland, en route to New York. The boy, traveling with his father, touched a control button on a motorized boarding ramp, causing it to smash into the plane's exit door. Passengers had to be shuttled to a hotel for an overnight stay while a three-man engineering crew was flown in from the United States to repair the damage.

Twenty-four hours later, 348 passengers reboarded Flight NW39 for New York. The boy and his father were asked to take a different flight home.

JOHNNY APPLESEED'S MISTAKE

As unlikely as it seems, Johnny Appleseed was an actual person. His real name was John Chapman, and he roamed from New England to Ohio at the beginning of the nineteenth century, barefoot and dressed in a burlap sack shirt and saucepan hat, planting apple trees wherever he went.

Unfortunately, apple trees are not his only legacy. Chapman was a great proponent of the medicinal properties of common plants, and he shared the common belief that dog fennel relieved fever. And so, along with apple pips, he spread dog fennel seeds across the countryside as he walked. The stubborn, foul-smelling weed plagues farmers to this day, and they refer to it, sardonically, as "Johnnyweed."

ARCHDUKE FERDINAND MEETS BUMBLING BOMB THROWERS

The wrong turns of history often have unexpected consequences, but few as calamitous as a wrong turn in Sarajevo in 1914.

In the early twentieth century Bosnia-Herzegovina was a province of the Austro-Hungarian empire and a hotbed of radical nationalism. For the most part, the radicals' revolutionary fervor was matched by their remarkable incompetence. In 1910 a Serbian law student fired five shots at the military governor; missing them all, he took his own life with his sixth. In 1912 a Croat student tried to shoot the administrative commissioner of Croatia but missed, wounding a secretary and killing a nearby policeman. There were two more failed attempts, in 1913 and 1914. Austria's Archduke Francis Ferdinand expected the same sort of welcome on his visit to Sarajevo. When his limousine had an engine fire the day before his departure, he muttered, "Here our car burns down and there they will throw bombs at us."

In Sarajevo the seven bumbling bomb throwers who planned to assassinate the archduke had gathered weeks before. They loudly hatched plots in beer halls crawling with police informants, and accidentally left a crate of weapons unattended for hours at a railway station. One got the date of the archduke's arrival by asking a police detective; another, Gavrilo Princip, dutifully registered his whereabouts with the police despite the fact that he was a well-known radical. Princip practiced with his pistol at a public park. Though Sarajevo was considered to be under heavy police repression at the time, none of this attracted any attention.

On June 28 the "assassins of a poorer quality" (as they were

described at their trial) stationed themselves along the Appel Quay beside the Miljacka River, and awaited the archduke's motorcade. As it passed, the first was unable to shoot because there was a gendarme nearby. The second felt sorry for the archduke's wife, Duchess Sophie, seated beside him, and couldn't go through with it. The third was obstructed by a passerby. The fourth, who was nearsighted, was unable to recognize the archduke. The fifth, Cabrinovic, also had difficulty spotting his target but asked a helpful policeman which car he was in and, after being told, threw his bomb. He missed. His bomb bounced off the back of the archduke's car and blew up under the car behind it, wounding two officers and several pedestrians. Cabrinovic manfully chomped down on a cyanide capsule and threw himself into the Miljacka River but was fished out by the police, none the worse for wear. "I am a Serb hero!" he shouted to his rescuers when asked to identify himself. "He must be insane," observed Archduke Francis Ferdinand.

The motorcade sped to the town hall, depriving the last two assassins of their chances. After the official ceremonies, the archduke decided to visit the wounded officers at the hospital on his return trip. The driver of the lead car didn't get the message, though, and turned up the wrong street off the Appel Quay with the motorcade following. Realizing the mistake, the archduke's driver stopped his car and began reversing back to the Appel Quay.

Meanwhile, Princip was moping around, disconsolate. All that target practice for nothing! Then he looked up and saw the archduke's car slowly backing down the street in front of him. Princip pulled out his gun, turned his head away and fired several shots at the archduke, killing him and the duchess.

As a result of the assassination, Austria-Hungary imposed demands on Serbia that led to war. Russia backed Serbia, and by August the allies of both sides had entered the fray. The shots that Gavrilo Princip fired not only ignited World War I but, indirectly, the Russian Revolution and World War II as well.

THE GOLDEN BANANA PEEL

The Golden Banana Peel shall be bestowed upon that individual who, in his or her utterances, consistently displays ignorance, illogic and obtuseness. The runners-up and winner will be announced in coming pages.
Nominees are:

Warren Austin, U.S. ambassador to the United Nations during the 1948 Arab-Israeli War, who said, "The only way we can hope to get anywhere is for the principals in this dispute to get together and talk this thing out as good Christians."

Charles Barkley of the Phoenix Suns, who angrily claimed he was misquoted in a new book about him. The book was his autobiography.

Yogi Berra, Yankee manager, who once said, "Baseball is ninety percent mental. The other half is physical."

Richard J. Daley, famed Chicago mayor, who had this to say regarding the "police riot" against antiwar protesters at the 1968 Democratic National Party Convention: "Get the thing straight once and for all. The policeman isn't there to create disorder; the policeman is there to preserve disorder."

Sam Goldwyn, the Hollywood producer, who once said, "I don't want any yes-man around me. I want everyone to tell me the truth even if it costs them their jobs!"

J. Edgar Hoover, who in June 1964 read a newspaper report

J. Edgar Hoover

that Jean-Paul Sartre, the famous French playwright and philosopher, had joined the "Who Killed Kennedy Committee," a group Hoover considered subversive. The newspaper identified Sartre only as an author, so the head of the FBI issued the following memo to his investigative staff: "Find out who **Sartre** is."

Shaquille O'Neal, who, after a visit to Athens, Greece, was asked if he had visited the Parthenon. "I can't really remember the names of all the clubs that we went to," he answered.

Dan Quayle, who once said, "One word sums up probably the responsibility of any vice president, and that one word is 'to be prepared.'"

Rev. William Archibald Spooner of Oxford University, master of verbal somersaults, who told his students during World War I, "When our boys come home from France, we will have the hags flung out."

Ted Turner, who, during a 1986 speech on world peace in Titusville, Florida, made the following contribution to international brotherhood and understanding: "Imagine the Italians at war. I mean, what a joke. They didn't belong in the last war, they were sorry they were in it, they were glad to get out of it. They'd rather be involved in crime and just making wine and having a good time..."

Raquel Welch, who for nearly a year thought the word gauche (French for clumsy or maladroit) meant cute. She greeted the sight of anything endearing with a perky "How gauche!"

While appearing on "The Larry King Show," Welch referred to the "51 states" of the United States. She stuck with the figure even after King gently corrected her.

ABSTRACT EXPRESSIONIST WOWS SWEDES

Swedish art gallery goers were impressed with the powerful brush strokes and dynamic color sense of a new abstract artist, Pierre Brassau. At a show in Göteborg, Sweden, in 1964, several paintings were sold for prices ranging up to $90.

The show had been arranged by a group of newspaper reporters because Pierre Brassau was in no position to handle it himself. He was behind bars at the time. That's where the zoo kept the four-year-old West African chimpanzee.

BUDDY BAKER'S WILD RIDE

A series of events worthy of a slapstick movie occurred at the Smoky Mountain Raceway in Tennessee on June 6, 1968.

Veteran driver Buddy Baker's Dodge blew out a tire on the first turn and slammed into a concrete wall. Suffering a slight concussion and broken ribs, Baker was strapped onto a rolling stretcher and loaded into an ambulance to be taken to the hospital. The ambulance driver, no doubt an aspiring racer himself, turned on his siren and put the pedal to the floor. Unfortunately, he had forgotten to latch the rear door. As the ambulance pulled out, the door flew open and the stretcher rolled out onto the track.

Baker was fully conscious at the time. "There I was strapped to this stretcher and it was rolling clean across the track on the back straightaway in front of everybody," Baker recalled. Terrified, he watched as the race cars—still driving around the track, though under the yellow caution flag—headed straight toward him. "I told myself, 'Ain't this something. Here I survive a crash head-on into a cement wall and now I'm gonna get killed on a rolling stretcher.'"

Fortunately, the driver of the pace car spotted the runaway stretcher patient and waved the other cars to the side of the track. They passed Baker, still rolling, as the medics ran up the track after him. Once they had caught up with him, Baker refused to be put back into the ambulance while strapped to the stretcher. Broken ribs or not, he insisted on riding in the passenger seat.

Like most professional drivers, Baker fears amateur drivers more than anything. He was more than a little alarmed as the ambulance driver ran wide open on his way to the hospital. The driver didn't even slow down for a red light and nearly collided with a car. Forced to swerve out of the car's way, the ambulance driver drove up onto a sidewalk and plowed through a row of garbage cans. The ambulance arrived at the emergency room running on one flat tire.

After Baker was patched up the ambulance crew offered to give him a lift back to the track, but he politely declined.

BABE RUTH BRONZE STRIKES OUT

A 9-foot, 800-pound bronze statue of Babe Ruth was erected at the entrance to Oriole Park in Baltimore, Maryland, in 1995. Every detail of the design had been scrutinized to ensure authenticity. Did he wear his belt buckle on the right side or the left? Did he wear his cap cocked to the side or straight? Exactly how big were the belt loops on his uniform?

It seemed no element of the likeness was too minor to escape scrutiny—except one. The Babe Ruth in the sculpture is holding a right-handed fielder's glove, and Babe was a lefty. The mistake was not discovered until the sculpture was complete.

Fans groaned. The Sultan of Swat batted left. Threw left. He'd even been called "Lefty" as a kid.

The artist, Susan Luery, admitted to "not being very astute in the finer points of sports."

STEREO DEALER GOES BANANAS

Advertisers should choose their words carefully—otherwise they may have to eat them. In 1986 Silo, a discount appliance-store chain, ran a TV commercial in Seattle and El Paso that offered a stereo system for only "299 bananas." Dozens of customers took the store at its word and lined up to purchase stereos with bags full of bananas.

Silo honored the deal and lost $10,465 on the campaign. Talk about stepping on a banana peel!

BASIC INSTINCT LOSES BY A TAIL

It's hard to imagine the frustration of fans who bet on Basic Instinct, the six-to-one favorite in an August 24, 1974, race at the Atlantic City Racetrack. The horse was led into the starting gate and the back stall door was closed behind him. When the starting gates clanged open, the horses broke cleanly and surged down the track—all of them, that is, but Basic Instinct, who remained at the gate. The horse's jockey, Carlos Barrera, kicked with his heels and smacked with his crop, but Basic Instinct refused to budge. He couldn't. The rear stall gate had been closed on his tail.

Money wagered on Basic Instinct was graciously refunded.

BATTLE OF NEW ORLEANS: BETTER LATE THAN NEVER

The Battle of New Orleans, in which Andrew Jackson's U.S. forces soundly defeated the British, was fought on January 8,

1815, two weeks after the Treaty of Ghent officially ended the War of 1812.

BEAR, STEARNS & CO. BLITZES WALL STREET

A ticker tape parade down New York City's Wall Street is a traditional honor for America's heroes. Of course, *real* ticker tape is passé; now they use computer paper. In 1984 Olympic medal winners were showered with tons of it, including hundreds of pages of accounts from the investment firm of Bear, Stearns & Co. Confidential printouts of clients' names, addresses and portfolio particulars were thrown from the company's offices into the street. Dozens of competing brokers scrambled to scoop up the files as if it was raining money—as indeed it was. One pinstriped trash picker walked away with over a hundred pages of valuable customer leads. Bear Stearns managing partner Alvin Einbender was more than a little chagrined. As he told the press, "I haven't caught the person who did it, but if I did and we were an Islamic country, we would probably punish him suitably."

THE BEATLES GET A THUMBS-DOWN

On New Year's Day, 1962, the Beatles had their first audition for a major label, the Decca Record Company in London. They felt they had done well, but a few weeks later their manager Brian Epstein received a call from Decca's Dick Rowe saying that the group would not be signed.

"Why?" asked Epstein.

"Not to mince words, Mr. Epstein, we don't like your boys' sound. Groups are out; four-piece groups with guitars particularly are finished," declared Rowe.

"The Beatles are going to be bigger than Elvis Presley," Epstein insisted, but it was futile. Decca had auditioned several bands on the same day as the Beatles, and Dick Rowe had decided that only one would be selected. He chose Brian Poole and the Tremelos because they lived nearer to London and it would be more convenient to work with them than with the Beatles, who were 200 miles away in Liverpool.

BELLY BUTTON ON THE SIDE

"A flat, sexy belly" was what Virginia O'Hare of Poughkeepsie,

New York, requested from plastic surgeon Howard Bellin. After the tummy tuck was performed in November 1974, O'Hare discovered that her belly button had been moved 2 inches off center. Dr. Bellin, who had previously done satisfactory work on O'Hare's nose and eyelids, insisted that the misplacement was a half-inch at most, which he considered "not cosmetically unacceptable." O'Hare did not agree, and filed a malpractice suit seeking millions for pain and suffering and loss of earnings, as well as corrective surgery to recenter her navel. She settled for $200,000.

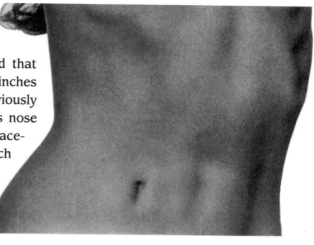

BIBLICAL BLUNDERS BEWILDER BELIEVERS

A Bible printed in England in 1631 by Barker and Lucas, the king's printers, offered readers an alternative to established norms of morality. In the Book of Exodus (20:14) the Ten Commandments were listed, with number seven coming out as: "Thou shalt commit adultery."

The printers had mistakenly omitted the word *not*.

Charles I, king at the time, recalled all 1,000 copies and fined the printers £3,000. It came to be known as the "Wicked Bible."

Other editions of the Bible are highly prized by collectors due to their "textual idiosyncrasies."

- The "Bug Bible" of 1551 got its name from an odd translation in the 91st Psalm. Instead of reading "Thou shalt not be afraid for the terror by night," it reads "Thou shalt not be afraid of any buggies by night."
- The "Breeches Bible" was printed in 1560. It got its name from its unique passage stating that Adam and Eve "sewed fig leaves together and made themselves breeches."
- The "Treacle Bible," printed in 1568, replaces the word "balm" with the word "treacle" in the line "Is there no balm in Gilead?"

Two other Bibles may have gotten the devil in them. A 1653 edition included the verses: "The fool hath said in his heart there is a God," and "Know ye not that the unrighteous shall inherit the Kingdom of God?" A 1716 edition changed "Sin no more" to the catchy "Sin on more."

Perhaps these pernicious typos caused the divine hand to change the word *Princes* to a more appropriate one in one edition of the Bible, which contains the verse "Printers have persecuted me without a cause."

We have to admire the dedication of the missionary who translated the Bible into an obscure Eskimo dialect, but inevitably mistakes were made. The biblical verse that reads "nation shall rise up against nation" (Mark 13:8) came out in the Eskimo version, due to one misplaced letter in a 17-letter word, as the perplexing "a pair of snowshoes shall rise up against a pair of snowshoes."

SENATOR BIDEN'S BOGUS BIO

Neil Kinnock, British Labor Party candidate for prime minister, delivered a stirring account of his humble background in May 1987:

"Why am I the first Kinnock in a thousand generations to be able to get to university?...Was it because our predecessors were thick?...Was it because they were weak, those people who could work eight hours underground and then come up and play football, weak?...It was because there was no platform on which they could stand."

Joe Biden, senator from Delaware and candidate for the Democratic Party nomination, delivered the following account of his own humble background in August 1987:

"Why is it that Joe Biden is the first in his family to go to university?...Is it because our fathers and mothers were not bright? Is it because they didn't work hard, my ancestors who worked in the coal mines and would come up after twelve hours and play football?...It's because they didn't have a platform on which to stand."

What do we learn from Senator Biden's account, aside from the fact that his ancestors worked 12 hours a day in the mines, unlike Mr. Kinnock's, who worked a mere eight? We learn that when you are trying to tout your character through an account of family history, it's generally better to stick with your own family history rather than that of someone else. Senator Biden left the race shortly after the similarity between his speech and that of Mr. Kinnock was discovered.

OOPS! SPECIAL SECTION: BILLION DOLLAR BLUNDERS

Any fool can lose a million, but it takes a financial genius to let a billion slip through his or her fingers. Here are four who did:

THE JARI PROJECT: UP THE CREEK

American billionaire Daniel K. Ludwig prided himself on his ability to recognize coming trends. Born poor in 1897, Ludwig made his fortune in the 1950s with supertankers and then diversified into mining, oil, ranching, gambling and real estate. In the 1960s he looked at the coming Information Age and saw a future in which paper would be in short supply. How to profit from that need? Ludwig had an extraordinary vision: He would buy up a huge tract in the Amazon rain forest, plant it with timber and produce pulp in his own plant on the site.

Ludwig had no trouble interesting the Brazilian government in the deal. In 1967 it sold him a plot roughly the size of Connecticut along the Jari River for less than one dollar an acre. Thirty-five thousand workers were hired to clear the jungle and lay 2,800 miles of road and 45 miles of railroad track. A city was built to house them.

It is hard to imagine the astonishment of Amazon dwellers watching what looked like two entire cities moving up the river in April 1978. These were the pulp mill and its power plant, built in Japan at a cost of $269 million and floated more than halfway around the world on barges. Each weighed 66 million pounds and was 250 yards long and 20 stories high. Too big to navigate the Panama Canal, the barges had to navigate around Africa's Cape of Good Hope.

Ecologists worried about the long-term effect of the massive operation on the rain forest, but Ludwig disputed their characterization of the jungle ecosystem as "fragile." As it turned out, the rain forest turned out to be perfectly capable of undoing the gargantuan plans of Daniel K. Ludwig. The melina trees imported from Indonesia failed to thrive in the sparse Amazonian soil. Termites and leaf-cutting ants ravaged crops and supplies. Workers were plagued with malaria and meningitis. By the late 1970s the Jari project was foundering, prey to what some have called the "Amazon factor": a merciless combination of climate, isolation, poor soil, insects and disease that has frustrated every effort to exploit the region's great potential.

In 1982 Ludwig, then 84 years old and in poor health, was forced to surrender. His project was taken over by Brazilians, who vastly scaled it back. Ludwig went into seclusion, his 15-year quest having set him back more than a billion dollars. He died in 1992, still a billionaire, but just barely.

THE HUNTS: THE MIDAS TOUCH IN REVERSE

Herbert and Bunker Hunt were two of the sons of H. L. Hunt, the eccentric billionaire oil man who kept three separate families going at the same time—three houses, three wives and 15 children. H.L. claimed he had a "genius gene" and felt obliged to spread it as far as possible. (H.L. also once said that he gave up smoking cigars because he had figured out that his time was worth $40,000 an hour, and he could no longer afford to waste any of it looking for matches.)

In the early seventies, shortly before their father's death, Herbert and Bunker Hunt began investing in silver, then selling it for $1.50 an ounce. When the value doubled shortly thereafter the brothers made a handsome profit, and the easy money gave them the speculating bug. Silver seemed like a good bet. It had numerous industrial and commercial uses, and it was a hedge against inflation. By 1973 the Hunts had taken possession of 55 million ounces of silver, valued at $160 million. Then the Hunts decided to corner the silver market, which they figured would be possible if they bought up 200 million ounces. Working in concert with wealthy Arabs, they began snapping up all the silver that came on the world market. By the end of the seventies they had 130 million ounces, with contracts for 90 million more.

Due to inflation, the Soviet invasion of Afghanistan and the demand created by the Hunts' own voracious purchases, the price of precious metals soared. In January 1980 silver sold for $50 an ounce, making the Hunts' holdings worth $4.5 billion, $3.5 billion more than they had paid for them. Fearing the effects of this dramatic price rise, the U.S. government put a limit to futures speculation in silver. The measures dropped the price to $21 an ounce by March 1980. Unable to meet the margin calls of $10 million a day on their silver futures, the Hunts teetered on the verge of financial collapse. The U.S. government had engineered their ruin, but now, concerned about market stability, stepped in to lend them $1.1 billion.

By 1986 the Hunts filed for bankruptcy protection under Chapter 11, having sustained losses of $1.5 billion. Bunker tried to put the best face on things with the blithe observation that "a billion dollars isn't what it used to be." Forced to sell their personal assets, by 1990 they were each left with a personal fortune of $1.5 million, less than one-tenth of 1% of what they were worth before they got the idea of cornering the world's silver market.

NICHOLAS LEESON: LOSING HIS BARINGS

The financial world was rocked in March 1995 when Barings, the 233-year-old British bank that had financed the Louisiana Purchase, the Napoleonic Wars and the tea shipment that was dumped in Boston Harbor, announced that it was forced to close its doors. What was even more astonishing was that the debacle had come about through the speculations of one person. Nicholas Leeson, a 28-year-old investor in its Singapore office, had cost the bank an estimated $1.38 billion.

Leeson started at Barings in 1989 and rose quickly with his special touch for index arbitrage, one of those financial instruments that is difficult for an outsider to understand and only sounds more confusing and absurd the more you learn about it. In 1992 Leeson and his wife, Lisa, who also worked for Barings, accepted a transfer to its Singapore office. There, Leeson was no longer under close adult supervision; his wife held the supervisory position that would normally have kept an eye on his dealings. Leeson began dealing in derivatives, specifically futures contracts based on the performance of the Nikkei index, the Tokyo Stock Exchange. Derivatives of this sort serve a purpose if used to hedge countervailing investments, but investing in them by themselves is as sensible as putting all your money on red at a roulette wheel.

In early 1995 the Nikkei index plunged 1,000 points after the Kobe earthquake and Leeson's bets went sour, leading him to pursue a classic roulette strategy. As one trader explained it, "You bet on red and you lose. You double your bet and you lose again. But as long as you keep doubling your bet, you will never lose in the end—as long as you have unlimited capital." Aye, there's the rub. Sooner or later you run out of money. Leeson had been concealing his errors in a secret computer file that made it look as if he was investing for a client, but when the time finally came to pay the bill, it arrived on Barings' doorstep. There wasn't enough in the cash drawer to cover it. As the axe fell, Leeson fled Singapore with his wife, leaving a note on his desk that simply read, "I'm sorry."

Leeson was dubbed a "rogue trader." In class-conscious England, much was made of his lower-class background, with mutterings that this is what you get when you put the wrong sort in charge. Others were astonished that so much financial clout could be wielded by someone in his 20s, only to be told that that's typical in the gladiatorial arena of high stakes investing, where a 40-year-old is considered over the hill. Lastly, most of us were surprised to learn that the highly speculative risks he had taken were unusual only in degree, not in kind; he would have been a hero if his gamble had paid off.

Now in jail, Leeson has been promised a $1 million advance for a book on the story. That would amount to less than one-tenth of 1% of the amount he lost. There was also a report that he had recorded a version of the Frank Sinatra standard, "My Way," but that turned out to be unfounded.

CITRON'S INVESTMENTS SQUEEZE JUICE FROM ORANGE COUNTY

On December 6, 1994, rich, Republican Orange County filed for bankruptcy five days after its investment pool announced a $1.7 billion loss. Robert Citron, the county's long-time treasurer who had put $8 billion of the county's funds in high-risk derivatives, was immediately fired. County administrators also blamed Merrill Lynch, suing the investment firm for $2 billion for negligence in selling Citron the risky investments. The county also sued its former auditor, Peat Marwick, for $3 billion for failing to warn it about its looming financial catastrophe. All the blame casting may have been defensive; a special investigation by the California State Senate concluded that Orange County elected officials were primarily responsible. The county had been living beyond its means for years, and Citron had been pressured to cover the tab. Before his luck ran out, Citron's investments were generating 35% of the its locally-generated revenue, compared to the 25% that came from property taxes. Many officials were aware of the risks involved, but preferred them to the political risk of cutting services or raising taxes, difficult to do under Prop 13.

In December 1995 it was revealed that Citron's investments had been based on advice given him by a mail order astrologer and a psychic. You would think that as Citron lost hundreds of millions his faith in fortune telling might be shaken, but he got at least one sound prediction. The psychic told him that December 1995 would be a very bad month.

BLOOPERS

New Yorker magazine has long prided itself on its meticulous fact checking, so a recent blooper was blamed on a "transcription service." In its editor's note section, it apologized to former Secretary of Education William Bennett for mangling a quote. It explained, "In criticizing the political views of Pat Buchanan, Mr. Bennett said, 'It's a real us-and-them kind of thing,' not, as we reported, 'It's a real S&M kind of thing.'"

The SouthWestern Bell Company's Yellow Pages mistakenly listed the Elliot-Hamil Funeral Home of Abilene, Texas, under "wholesale frozen foods."

"Lake Como [Italy], its shore dwellers like to say, is shaped like a man striding westward, his front foot in Como and the other in Lecco. Between the two legs is a promontory of great beauty..."   —Franc Shor in *National Geographic*, July 1968

GQ magazine quoted former marine and defense attorney F. Lee Bailey as saying, "On weekends I like to wear ballet shoes: They're light and dressy." The quote was improperly transcribed; Bailey had actually said he favored Bally brand shoes.

Harry von Zell, announcer for the old Burns and Allen radio show, once introduced the president before a nationwide radio address by saying: "Ladies and gentlemen, the president of the United States, Hoobert Heever."

BOSTON STRANGLER HONORED BY TEXAS

The Boston Strangler, Albert de Salva, who confessed to killing 13 women in the Boston area, was officially honored in the Texas State House in 1971 for his pioneering work in population control. The resolution commending de Salva was introduced by Texas state representative Tom Moore, Jr., who hoped to show how little attention legislators paid to many of the bills they voted on.

The bill commended the Boston Strangler for serving "his country, his state, and his community...This compassionate gentleman's dedication and devotion to his work has enabled the weak and lonely throughout the nation to achieve and maintain a new degree of concern for their future...He has been officially recognized by the state of Massachusetts for his noted activities and unconventional techniques involving population control and applied psychology."

The resolution passed unanimously.

BOXER BINGES, BLOWS BOUT

A large meal cost a South African boxer a chance for a medal at the 1936 Olympic Games in Berlin.

The boxer, Hamilton-Brown, lost an opening-round bout on a split decision. Crushed to have lost so quickly after months of rigorous training, discipline and self-denial, Hamilton-Brown consoled himself with a night of binge eating.

Meanwhile, one of the judges discovered that he had reversed two of his scores and had actually intended to declare the South African the winner. Hamilton-Brown was still in contention and was scheduled to fight the next day. Unfortunately, his coach was not able to locate him until midnight, by which time his overindulgence had done its work. The boxer had gained 5 pounds, pushing him over the limit for his weight class. Desperate measures were no doubt tried, but he was unable to lose the necessary weight before his next bout and was disqualified.

A BRIDGE TOO SMALL

In 1981, when the Intermarine company of Ameglia, Italy, won a large shipbuilding contract from the government of Malaysia, observers were surprised. Intermarine specialized in building vessels far smaller than the minesweeper and three military launches the order called for. Nevertheless, it completed the ships within two years as promised. It was only then that a problem became apparent. Intermarine's shipyard was a mile from the Mediterranean on the Magra River, and the river was crossed by the lovely but diminutive Colombiera Bridge. Not one of the ships could pass under it. The shipyard offered to take apart the bridge and reconstruct it after the ships had passed, but the local council refused.

BUSH'S UNDIPLOMATIC LUNCHEON

In January of 1992 President Bush was in Tokyo seeking trade concessions from Japan's leaders. While at a state dinner, he took the unprecedented diplomatic initiative of vomiting directly into the lap of prime minister Kiichi Miyazawa. Bush, who was suffering from an intestinal flu, then collapsed onto the Prime Minister. He reportedly remarked gamely, "Why don't you just roll me under the table and let me sleep it off?"

The move impressed the Japanese sufficiently to make some concessions. It also contributed a new expression to the Japanese language: "Bushuru," to lose one's lunch publicly and under embarrassing circumstances. In Japan, where heavy drinking at bars is a common after-work activity, the expression fills a linguistic need. A Japanese comedy program even featured a monkey trained to feign vomiting, complete with realistic retching sounds, whenever it heard the word *Bushuru*.

BUSH, GEORGE; THE WIT AND WISDOM OF

While campaigning in 1988, George Bush repeatedly stressed his close relationship with Reagan. At one appearance in Twin Falls, Idaho, he boasted that he and Reagan "have had triumphs, we have made mistakes, we have had sex."

Decrying the views of eight campaign aides who resigned under accusations of anti-Semitism, George Bush proudly declared, "I hope I stand for anti-bigotry, anti-Semitism, anti-racism. That is what drives me."

Addressing the Louisville, Kentucky, chapter of the American Legion on September 7, Bush jumped the gun by three months when he told the startled veterans, "Today is Pearl Harbor Day. Forty-seven years ago to this very day, we were hit and hit hard at Pearl Harbor."

OLDEST LIVING HUMAN ACES REAL ESTATE DEAL

For the right to take possession of 90-year-old Jeanne Calment's handsome Arles apartment upon her death, French lawyer André-François Raffray arranged to pay her a $500-a-month annuity. Actuarial tables would suggest that he had made a shrewd investment, but no. The deal was made known when Jeanne Calment celebrated her 120th birthday, and she became known to be the oldest person on earth. Mrs. Calment reported that she sent Raffray a card every year on her birthday on which she wrote, "Sorry, I'm still alive."

Mr. Raffray died at the age of 77 in December 1995, having paid Mrs. Calment a total of $184,000, almost three times the apartment's value. He's still not off the hook. Under the agreement, his estate has to continue paying Mrs. Calment as long as she lives. "In life, one sometimes makes bad deals," Calment observed philosophically of her lawyer's plight.

Jay Leno suggested that the story proves that nothing gives people the will to live more than knowing that they're screwing a lawyer.

HUMAN CANNONBALL BLOWS TOP

"Rita Thunderbird" was the stage name of a human cannonball. Clad in a gold lamé bikini, she slipped into the cannon's muzzle in 1977 for a performance in Battersea, England. When the cannon was fired, Miss Thunderbird remained lodged in the barrel, but her bikini top was shot across the Thames River.

D DAY IN THE DARKROOM

"If your pictures are no good, you aren't close enough," said Robert Capa, *Life* magazine's premier combat photographer during World War II. True to his words, Capa hit the beach in Normandy with E Company in the first wave on D Day. Terrified by machine-gun fire and artillery bursts, with GIs dying all around him, Capa shot two 36-exposure rolls before retreating, exhausted, to a landing craft. The bridge of the craft took a direct hit, and Capa found himself covered, inexplicably, with feathers. He realized they were from the stuffing of the flotation vests of men that had just been blown up. Capa made it safely back to the ship in another landing craft.

Back in England, his film had to be processed quickly and flown to New York in order to meet *Life*'s publishing deadline. When the negatives were developed, it was clear that they were all everyone had hoped for. Feeling that the whole world was waiting to see these pictures, John Morris, *Life*'s London picture editor, ordered the photo lab, "Rush me prints!"

The lab technician set the film drying cabinet on high, and melted the celluloid base of the negatives. All the photos except for 11 were ruined. Those that survived were blurred but are still considered the finest photos taken of the invasion.

The actual cause of the loss of his pictures was concealed from Capa for weeks; he was told that seawater had seeped into his cameras and spoiled the film. Whoever finally broke the truth to him must have been very, very brave.

CAROLINO'S *THE NEW GUIDE OF THE CONVERSATION IN PORTUGUESE AND ENGLISH*, OR *ENGLISH AS SHE IS SPOKE.*

Some grasp of the English language would seem to be a minimal qualification to author an English-language phrase book. Pedro Carolino, a Portuguese author, did not meet this qualification but proceeded undeterred. Though he did not possess an English-Portuguese dictionary, Carolino made do with a Portuguese-French dictionary and a French-English dictionary.

In 1815 he published *The New Guide of the Conversation in Portuguese and English*, which was subsequently reprinted under the title *English As She Is Spoke*.

The preface ends with the touching sentiment, "We expect then, who the little book (for he care that we wrote him, and for her typographical correction) that may be worth the acceptation of the studious persons, and especially of the youth, at which we dedicate him particularly."

The book begins with some "Familiar Phrases" that the Portuguese traveler might find useful, among them:

"She make the prude."

"Do you cut the hairs?"

"You hear the bird gurgling?"

In the chapter of "Familiar Dialogues," dialogue 18—"For to ride a horse"—begins with this admonition to a stable keeper obviously trying to take advantage of the traveler:

"Here is a horse who have bad looks. Give me another. I will not that. He not sall how to march, he is pursy, he is foundered. Don't you are ashamed to give me a jade as like? He is undshoed, he is with nails up."

In a section with the intriguing title of "Idiotisms and Proverbs," Carolino provides his readers with a selection of the aphorisms they would be likely to encounter on even the briefest visit to an English-speaking country:

"Nothing some money, nothing of Swiss."

"He eat to coaches."

"A take is better than two you shall have."

Al Capone

Carolino's book came to be recognized as a work of inadvertent comic genius, and a 60-page pamphlet of selections, published in England in 1883, went through 10 editions. Mark Twain was a devoted fan of Carolino, and predicted that "this celebrated phrase book will never die while the English language lasts."

THE SECRET OF CAPONE'S VAULT

Prior to his current incarnation as a TV schlockmeister, Geraldo Rivera enjoyed some reputation as a shamelessly self-promoting investigative journalist. In April 1986 Geraldo hosted a live two-hour broadcast from the basement of the Lexington Hotel in Chicago. A doorless, cement-walled room had been discovered, and was believed to be Al Capone's secret vault. It was going to be opened up and its contents revealed on national TV. Suspense was provided by the fact that it could contain anything, from stashes of cash, jewelry, booze or crates of bootleg whisky, to the moldering skeletons of disloyal business associates. Reporters were on hand for the event, as well as agents of the Internal Revenue Service, still looking for the $800,000 Capone owed them at the time of his death. While the vault was being blasted open, Geraldo kept things hopping by firing a Prohibition-era Thompson submachine gun and detonating a dynamite charge using an old-fashioned plunger.

It took technicians an hour and a half to blast their way into the vault. When at last entry was achieved and the dust settled down, the camera crew went in. Viewers who had stayed with the program were rewarded with a close-up of the contents of Capone's vault: two empty gin bottles. To help fill the remaining time, Geraldo sang "Chicago."

CARTER SPEECH PERPLEXES POLES

When President Carter visited Poland in 1977, he addressed an assembled crowd of 500 VIPs and government officials upon his arrival at the Warsaw airport. His speech is not remembered for the banal pleasantries he meant to deliver, but for the bizarre way the speech was mangled by State Department translator Steven Seymour, who spoke a strange, ungrammatical mixture of archaic Polish with Russian.

Carter opened with an innocent comment about his flight from Washington that morning. After translation, Poles were startled to hear Carter say that he had "left America, never to return."

When Carter said, "Our nation was founded," it came out as "Our nation was woven."

Mr. Seymour turned an innocuous comment by Carter on the Polish Constitution into "The Polish Constitution is a subject of ridicule."

Carter tried to tell the Poles, "I understand your hopes for the future." It came out as "I know your lusts for the future."

But all in all, the assembled Poles understood that Carter

regarded their people highly, and wished to enjoy a close, intimate relationship with them. At least, let's hope that's what they inferred when his statement "I have come to learn your opinions and understand your desires for the future," came out as "I desire the Poles carnally." The following day Mr. Seymour was assigned to other duties.

FAREWELL PARTY FOR CATHERINE THE GREAT'S TEA SERVICE

For high-ranking bureaucrats in the old USSR nearly any special privilege was available. The mayor of Leningrad (now St. Petersburg) wanted nothing but the best for his daughter's wedding in January 1980. He used his clout to get the Hermitage Museum, which stores many of the nation's art treasures, to let him use Catherine the Great's china tea set for the occasion.

As the evening wore on, and the guests grew more exuberant, one reveler got to his feet and accidentally dropped one of the priceless teacups. Assuming that he had proposed a toast, the rest of the guests took this as a signal for the traditional Russian gesture of good luck, stood up and threw their teacups into the fireplace, smashing them.

PARTIES GONE OUT OF BOUNDS

For eight years Iraq fought Iran. When the war finally ended at midnight on August 20, 1988, Iraqis celebrated by firing pistols and assault rifles into the air for three days.

As a result of spent bullets falling back to earth, 350 people were killed. This was more Iraqis than had been killed during the Iranian missile attacks on Baghdad earlier in the year.

In Karachi, Pakistan, revelers at a wedding who fired their rifles into the air brought down a Pakistan International Airlines plane, killing 13 passengers and injuring more than 20. The seven groomsmen were charged with "lethal celebrations during marriage ceremonies."

Soccer fans in the village of Ixiamas, Bolivia, threw firecrackers into the air to celebrate their country's victory in a World Cup qualifying match in 1993. The firecrackers fell back onto the thatched roofs of their huts, setting them on fire and burning almost the entire village to the ground.

PARADISE AT £500 A NIGHT

Dr. James Graham was centuries ahead of his time, addressing sexual problems in eighteenth-century London at his "Temple of Health." Graham was a great believer in his work, though the crowds of men who attended his lectures did so mainly out of interest in the scantily clad models he used as props for his lectures. Most popular were talks in which Emma Hart, the free-spirited society beauty who later became Admiral Nelson's mistress, served as a visual aid. The "Rosy Goddess of Health," as she was called, had no reservations about appearing in the nude to advance the cause of science, on one occasion demonstrating to an entranced audience how to take a healthful mud bath.

Graham invested his lecturing income in his great scientific breakthrough—the Celestial Bed. This magnificent piece of furniture measured 12 feet by 9, stood on eight brass legs and was decorated with carved cupids. It was available for rent to infertile couples at a princely £500 per night, and was supposed to maximize the odds that they would conceive a child. The sheets were silk and the mattress stuffed not with ordinary horsehair, but only with hair from selected stallions. Magnets were attached all around the bed, keeping the energy "continually pouring forth in an everlasting circle." The bed could even tilt, if need be. The rental fee included the services of a small orchestra to provide suitable background music.

Graham is reported to have invested £10,000 in his wondrous bed, a staggering sum at the time. It was the ruin of him. He died penniless in 1794.

CHRISTMAS IN TOKYO

Christmas has been enthusiastically embraced as a consumer event in Japan, complete with the Western trappings. However, since the holiday symbols have no religious or historical significance to the Japanese, they can get somewhat confused in the transition. In the early 1980s one Tokyo store decided to outdo the competition with its expression of the Christmas spirit. It erected a giant cross on the front of its building. On the cross, crucified, was none other than Santa Claus.

CHUTZPAH DEFINED

"I just pray to God the U.K. government spends their North Sea oil revenue intelligently, instead of continuing to pour money into subsidizing businesses that are losers from day one."
—John Z. DeLorean, speaking to the BBC on July 15, 1979. His DeLorean Motor Works later took the U.K. government for upwards of £50 million.

THE SECRET MESSAGE
OF THE CLINTON HEALTH CARE PLAN

When the Clinton administration's health care plan was released to the press, reporters had the option of getting it on computer disk. When they installed the disks, those who had virus-detection programs on their systems were warned that the disk contained the computer virus known as Stoned III. This virus flashes on the user's screen the message: "Your PC is stoned: LEGALIZE MARIJUANA."

The Clinton administration denied that the virus was on the master disks when they left the White House, and declared that it must have been added during the copying process.

CLINTON ADMINISTRATION,
LEAST SIGNIFICANT BLUNDERS OF THE

At a meeting of the heads of state of the seven top industrial nations in Brussels, Belgium, Bill Clinton greeted the 280-pound

German chancellor Helmut Kohl with the suave comment, "I was thinking of you last night, Helmut, because I watched the sumo wrestling on television."

While appearing on "Larry King Live," Al Gore failed to recognize his wife's voice when she called up, complimented him on his looks and asked, "Are you available for a date sometime?"

COFFEE VS. TEA—SWEDISH EXPERIMENT UPSETS THEORY

Gustav III, the eighteenth-century king of Sweden, believed that coffee was poisonous. In order to prove his theory, he conducted a long-term experiment on two murderers sentenced to death. Each was pardoned, one on the condition that he drink tea every day for the rest of his life, and the other on the condition that he drink coffee. Gustav then appointed two doctors to oversee the experiment and to see which of the subjects died first.

The doctors died first. Then King Gustav was assassinated in 1792 at the age of 46. Many years later, one of the murderers died at the age of 83. The tea drinker.

COLUMBUS, CHRISTOPHER; *ESQUIRE*'S "DUBIOUS MAN OF THE MILLENNIUM"

Each January *Esquire* magazine takes a sardonic look at the past year as it bestows its "Dubious Achievement Awards." In 1992, the quincentennial of Christopher Columbus' arrival in the New World, it considered the record of the great explorer and pronounced him the "Dubious Man of the Millennium." Why such disrespect?

- The only reason he felt confident he could reach the Indies was that he had underestimated the earth's circumference by 7,600 miles.
- The continent he "discovered" had previously been visited by the Vikings, and already had a population of millions.
- Even after four trips he insisted he had reached Asia and never believed he had found a New World, going so far as to refer to its inhabitants as "Indians."
- Though he opened up the territory to colonization, it was not named for him but for a less significant explorer, one who had the wit to realize he was in a place Europeans did not yet have a name for.

- On one voyage he was arrested for "malfeasance of governance" and returned to Spain in chains. On another, he claimed to have discovered the portal to the Garden of Eden.
- He searched desperately for gold and treasures but never found any.
- His crew introduced smallpox to the natives, and probably brought syphilis back to Europe in exchange.
- He was portrayed in a movie by Gérard Depardieu.

CANCER CONQUERS THE CONQUEROR

Every connoisseur of bad movies has a special fondness for *The Conqueror* (1956), Howard Hughes' epic about Genghis Khan. Its failings are many, but the first occurred in the casting. Susan Hayward was hired for the lead female role, as a hot-blooded Tartar princess. With her red hair and Irish beauty, this was an odd choice, but no matter—it paled beside the stupefying selection of John Wayne as Genghis Khan, which the *L.A. Times* described as history's "most improbable piece of casting unless Mickey Rooney were to play Jesus in *The King of Kings*." Wayne was never very convincing playing anyone but himself, and how he could be expected to pull off the part of the Mongol warlord was beyond comprehension. Nevertheless, the Duke was desperate for the part, which he felt was "the role of a lifetime," and, since he was at the peak of his box office appeal, director Dick Powell was glad to have him. To prove his seriousness,

Wayne dieted, took fencing lessons and worked with a dialogue coach.

Despite his best efforts, Wayne's mangling of the film's mock-Shakespearean language made the movie an instant camp classic. Several scenes stick in the mind. John Wayne wooing Hayward: "Yer bee-yootiful in yer wrath!...I shall keep you, and, in responding to my passions, yer hatred will kindle into love!" John Wayne speaking of her to his blood brother: "She is a wuh-man—*much* wuh-man! Should her perfidy be less than that of other wimmen?"

Nevertheless, it is not the movie's badness that rates it in this collection of astonishing blunders. It is the fact that the movie was filmed on location at Snow Canyon in the Utah desert, just 137 miles from the army's atomic bomb test site at Yucca Flat, Nevada. The canyon acted as a sort of dust trap for radioactive fallout. During the early fifties, no one thought much about the dangers of radiation, and the whole matter was a joke to the cast and crew. Thirty years later, of the 220 people who worked on location on *The Conqueror*, 91 had developed cancer and 46 had died from it, including John Wayne, Susan Hayward and Dick Powell.

CAPTAIN COOK OVERSTAYS HIS HAWAIIAN HOLIDAY

Most of us were taught as children not to overstay our welcome. The wisdom of that advice was certainly brought home to the

English explorer Captain James Cook by the Hawaiians.

In 1779, when Cook anchored his ship *Resolution* in Kealakekua Bay on Hawaii's west coast, he was accorded a tumultuous welcome by the natives there. Due to a number of extraordinary coincidences Cook was accepted as the great god Lono, returning at last. As had been prophesied, Cook came from a clockwise direction, at the proper time of the year, bearing extraordinary gifts (hatchets and nails). The masts and sails of his ships even resembled the crossbars and pennants that the natives carried in the annual festival honoring their god.

Cook knew nothing of this, of course, and could only wonder at Hawaiian hospitality. He was given gifts worthy of a deity, such as a cape made from the bright red feathers of a rare bird, and a plumed helmet. Day after day, he and his men were feasted and entertained.

After about two weeks the hospitality began to wear thin. The guests were expensive to maintain and not as godlike as the Hawaiians had hoped.

Feeling the mood, Cook and his men set sail. They hadn't gotten far when a storm blew up and broke the *Resolution's* foremast. They made the mistake of putting back into harbor for repair. This was too much for the Hawaiians. After a few nasty skirmishes, Cook was knocked down by the natives, held underwater and repeatedly stabbed until dead.

COOKBOOK OFFERS RECIPE FOR DISASTER

The full print run of the *Woman's Day Crockery Cuisine* cookbook, published in 1978, had to be recalled by Random House. It was discovered that the recipe for "silky caramel slices," which called for heating an unopened can of condensed milk in a Crock-Pot, could cause a life-threatening explosion. The publishers had forgotten to mention that the pot must first be filled with water.

CRITICS WITHOUT A CLUE

"Try another profession. Any other profession."
—An instructor at the John Murray Anderson Drama School to Lucille Ball in 1927

"Shakespeare's name, you may depend on it, stands absurdly too high and will go down."
—Lord Byron, 1814

"The Beatles? They're on the wane."
—The Duke of Edinburgh, giving his opinion while visiting Canada in 1965

"I'm sorry, Mr. Kipling, but you just don't know how to use the English language."
—From the *San Francisco Examiner's* 1889 rejection letter to Rudyard Kipling

"Losing hair. Can't sing. Can dance a little."
—Assessment of Fred Astaire's first screen test

"Far too noisy, my dear Mozart. Far too many notes."
—Emperor Ferdinand's reaction after the premiere performance of *The Marriage of Figaro*

"Rembrandt is not to be compared in the painting of character with our extraordinarily gifted English artist, Mr. Rippingille."
—John Hunt (1775-1848)

AUTOMOBILE INVENTOR LOSES LICENSE

French artillery officer Nicholas Cugnot designed and built a three-wheeled vehicle in 1769. It had front-wheel drive, powered by a two-piston steam engine. Cugnot claimed it could carry four people at a speed of 2 miles per hour. Unfortunately, the heavy copper boiler mounted on the front made steering difficult, and on its initial tryout it crashed into a brick wall, demolishing the car. In addition to being the world's first driver, Cugnot enjoyed the distinction of having the world's first automobile accident.

Though his contraption was damaged, Cugnot was not, and he set about building a larger version for the French War Ministry. He demonstrated the new model on a Paris street, but once again his steering let him down and he rolled over. The army lost interest, his vehicle was impounded and Cugnot achieved another first—he was the first motorist jailed for dangerous driving.

THE DALTON GANG'S LAST RAID

Bob, Emmett and Gratton Dalton were cousins of the Younger brothers, who rode with the James gang, and they grew up in Coffeyville, Kansas, where Jesse James was a hero. Eager to cut their own swath though outlaw history, the Daltons formed a gang and pulled off a number of train robberies. On the verge of retiring, they wanted to pull off one last really big job, one that would immortalize them. The plan, calculated to produce as much publicity as plunder, was to rob two banks in the same town at the same time, and the town they chose was Coffeyville, Kansas. Since it was their home turf, the Daltons didn't feel that any advance reconnaissance was called for. However, as they were well-known desperadoes throughout the area, disguises were definitely in order. On the morning of October 5, 1892, the three Daltons and two henchmen loaded up their weaponry, donned fake beards and rode into town. They dismounted, split up and headed toward their objectives, each carrying two six-shooters and a rifle. The weaponry caused little stir in the rough-and-tumble western town, but their obviously fake beards did. A local man, Charley Gump, recognized them and called out the alarm, causing Bob Dalton to take a shot at him. Before they'd even gotten into their respective banks, the Daltons had aroused the town. Once inside the Condon Bank, a teller told the holdup men that the safe had a time lock and couldn't be opened for three more minutes. So they waited.

Bear in mind that this was before the days of the Federal

Deposit Insurance Company. If your bank was robbed, you lost your money. Folks in the Old West didn't take kindly to that. The local hardware store passed out arms and ammunition to the townsfolk and an enormous gun battle broke out.

Aftermath of the great raid: (left to right) Bill Powers, Bob Dalton, Grat Dalton, Dick Broadwell.

The Dalton gang achieved its immortality—for mounting the most badly bungled bank robbery in western history. Two of the Daltons and both their henchmen were killed. Emmett Dalton, the sole survivor, was badly wounded and served 15 years in prison.

DEATH BE NOT STUPID

Lest we derive any morbid amusement from the accounts that follow, let us keep in mind the words of a spokesman for the National Funeral Directors' Association, who once observed that "death, especially to the person who has experienced it, is not funny."

Aeschylus, the father of Greek tragedy, met a somewhat comic end, according to historical accounts. He had been warned by a soothsayer that he would be killed one day by a falling object. After retiring to Sicily in 456 B.C. at the age of 69, he was walking across a wheat field when he was struck on the head by a falling tortoise and was instantly killed. It was apparently dropped by a high-flying eagle that mistook Aeschylus' bald head for a rock, on which it sought to break open the tortoise's shell.

Li Po, the great Chinese poet, composed his best work while thoroughly soused. His patron, Emperor Ming Huang, would transcribe his words, since the poet was incapable of writing while in that state. One night in A.D. 762, while boating, a well-lubed Li Po tried to kiss the reflection of the moon in the water, fell in and drowned.

The Chinese are renowned for their herbal remedies. The great Chinese practitioner Liu Pi brewed up an antiaging medicine and presented it to the Tang emperor Hsien Tsung. The emperor drank it and immediately died.

King Charles VIII of France was so afraid of being poisoned that he ate very little. He died of malnutrition.

The beard of Hans Steininger was longer than he was tall, and was believed to be the longest in the world. In September 1567, while climbing the steps leading to the council chamber in Brunn, Austria, Steininger tripped over his beard, fell down the stairs and died.

From his position as a violinist in Louis XIV's court band, Jean-Baptiste Lully rose to become the official composer for the French king. He created a new and original operatic style, which was widely imitated throughout Europe.

When Lully conducted an orchestra, he liked to keep time by tapping his long, pointed staff on the floor. While conducting the Te Deum for the king, he missed the floor, stabbed his own foot with his staff and died soon afterward from blood poisoning.

Moses Alexander, 93, married Frances Tompkins, 105, on June 11, 1831, in Bath, New York. The next morning they were found dead in bed.

Bobby Leach, a professional daredevil who'd survived going over Niagara Falls in a barrel in 1911, died 15 years later from injuries sustained when he slipped and fell on an orange peel.

David Grundman thought he'd have some fun at the expense

of a giant saguaro cactus in the desert near Phoenix, Arizona. He fired two shotgun blasts into the cactus, causing a 23-foot section to fall, crushing him.

"It was a human error and we are very, very sorry about the accident," said Jack Kennedy, spokesman for Vanderbilt Hospital in Nashville, Tennessee, after an 81-year-old man awaiting a routine operation died when a hospital worker accidentally administered him liquid air freshener instead of his medication.

The actress Barbara Bain, best known for her roles on "Mission: Impossible" and "Space: 1999," kept a small mutt named Socks as a pet for 14 years. The dog was sleeping on her front porch one day when the paper boy flung the heavy Sunday edition of the Los Angeles Times onto the porch, killing the dog.
The *Times* offered to pay for the dog, but Bain declined.

On the day in 1986 on which Japan's mandatory seat-belt law went into effect, Fumietsu Okubo, 65, was strangled to death after becoming tangled in his shoulder harness.

DELPHIC ORACLE IS RIGHT AGAIN
Ancient Greeks visited the oracle at Delphi in search of guidance. Enveloped in intoxicating fumes emitted from a crack in the earth, the crones who sat in the temple delivered prophesies that were often ambiguous.
Croesus, the richest monarch of his time, sought the oracle's advice as to whether he should go to war against Cyrus the Great, king of Persia. The oracle told him that when he went to war he "would destroy a great empire." Croesus was heartened and rewarded the temple with 117 bricks of precious metals, a statue of a lion made of 570 pounds of gold, and other treasures with a total value of over a billion dollars in today's terms.
Croesus went merrily to war, but his army was crushed. As prophesied, he had indeed destroyed a great empire—he just hadn't anticipated that it would be his own.

IF GOD HAD WANTED US TO VOTE, HE WOULD HAVE GIVEN US CANDIDATES...

In 1928 Liberian president Charles King decided to put his popularity to the test of a popular vote. Afterward he was gratified to be able to announce that he had been reelected with an officially counted 600,000-vote majority.

King's opponent in the election, Thomas Faulkner, complained that the election had been rigged. Challenged to substantiate his allegations, Faulkner pointed out that it was difficult to obtain a 600,000-vote margin with an electorate of less than 15,000.

During the 1967 mayoral election in Picoaza, Ecuador, a foot-powder manufacturer ran an ad campaign for his product, Pulvapies, with the slogan, "Vote for any candidate, but if you want well-being and hygiene, vote for Pulvapies."

When the polls were closed and the votes counted, it turned out that Pulvapies had been elected by a substantial margin.

Running for the Republican presidential nomination in 1980, former Texas governor John Connally invested 14 months and $12 million of his own money. He managed to win a single delegate to the Republican convention, Mrs. Ada Mills of Clarksville, Arkansas. Mrs. Mills was known as the "$12 million Delegate."

Seven years later Connally declared bankruptcy.

Even allowing for inflation, Michael Huffington outdid Connally in his unsuccessful 1994 senatorial bid, spending $28 million of his own money in the California race. Understandably, Huffington was reluctant to concede defeat to the winner, Dianne Feinstein, even weeks after the returns were in.

BUMPY TAKEOFF FOR THE DENVER INTERNATIONAL AIRPORT

Frederico Peña, former Denver mayor and Secretary of Transportation under Clinton, billed the Denver International Airport as "an airport of the twenty-first century." If so, the next 100 years are going to be rough.

First, we heard about problems with the $232 million automated baggage-handling system. It displayed a tendency to chew up and swallow people's luggage. When the $4.7 billion airport finally opened for service on February 28, 1995, 16 months past schedule and $3 billion over budget, it was not to universal acclaim. Critics complained that, at 25 miles, the airport is too far from Denver. Cab fare is so high ($76 round-trip) that many people find it cheaper to rent a car to get to and from the airport. Not that it's easy to rent a car at DIA. Rental car lots are 5 miles away, and Hertz advises passengers to drop off their cars at least 90 minutes before their flight time. The ultramodern control tower was designed to be able to operate in severe weather, but when it rains the roof leaks, causing ceiling tiles to fall on air traffic controllers, who have to cover their computer terminals with plastic sheeting. The runways, built on unstable soil, frequently crack and have to be repaired with industrial-strength glue. To add insult to injury, the multipeaked design of the passenger terminal was likened to a circus tent draped over a big hedgehog.

To help alleviate its massive debt, DIA has a per-customer cost of $18.50, more than twice that of other airports, a cost that has to be passed along to travelers. This has caused many airlines to shun the terminal, and many travelers choose to route themselves through the more convenient Colorado Springs Airport, which has enjoyed a 7% gain in traffic since DIA opened. Continental Airlines, which had used Denver as its hub, pulled out, taking 5,000 jobs from the area.

As Denver mayor from 1983 to 1991, Frederico Peña was the guiding force behind the DIA; in fact, the road leading up to it is named Peña Boulevard. Former Colorado governor Richard Lamm said he had cautioned against what has become the largest single-site public works project in the country, but "[Peña] wanted to be associated with some solution to the airport problem." Some solution. One Denver attorney, quoted in the *Wall Street Journal*, said, "It's an airport we didn't need and can't afford."

In fact, in a November trip to the area, President Clinton chose to land Air Force One at Colorado Springs rather than risk the curse of DIA. A curse, you ask? Well, DIA was built on land sacred to local Indian tribes, but surely that has nothing to do with all this...

NO DIGNITY FOR THE DEPARTED

The body parts of renowned figures and great geniuses were sometimes removed for ceremonial purposes or special study. There was no guarantee that they would be treated with proper respect, however.

- Voltaire's brain was accidentally left in a chest of drawers, which was auctioned off in a furniture sale at the Hotel Drouot in Paris.
- Along with household trash, Talleyrand's preserved brain was mistakenly dumped into the sewer in front of his mansion.
- Cleopatra's mummified remains had been kept in a Paris museum since Napoleon looted them from Egypt, left behind when other Egyptian artifacts were returned. In the 1940s workmen cleaning the museum dumped the contents of a mummy case into the sewers. The mummy case was later identified as Cleopatra's.

DEPARTMENT OF CORRECTIONS CORRECTS CALLERS

A survey conducted by the California Department of Corrections revealed that 20% of the population believe that the purpose of the department is to solve problems and to get things fixed. Similar surveys in other states indicate that this misapprehension holds true nationwide. Departments of Corrections routinely receive calls from citizens wishing to have help with Social Security check mix-ups and building code violations. Many of these callers are unpersuaded when they are told the actual meaning of "Corrections."

Some people just don't understand a euphemism when they hear one.

DESERTER PICKS PIGSTY OVER PRISON

During World War II Soviet army deserters were shot or sent to die in the gulags, causing many to hide from the authorities for years after the war ended. Those who turned up decades after hostilities had ended were routinely pardoned, being regarded as more pathetic than traitorous. One collaborator gave himself up in 1962, having spent 20 years hiding under a bed, only to find out he'd been officially pardoned five years before. In 1966 a deserter believed to have been killed in the Battle of Stalingrad left his brother's house where he'd hidden for 24 years, never having informed his wife and daughter that he was still alive. Another deserter held out for 30 years in a barn in the Ukraine. None were charged with any wrongdoing.

Pavel Navrotsky surrendered to the Germans when they swept across the Ukraine in 1941. They sent him home, where he remained until Soviet troops recaptured the area in 1944. Afraid of retribution, Navrotsky took refuge in a pigsty in his yard. His wife secretly fed him and kept the door padlocked. He only left his hideout once, when he went out for a walk late at night disguised in a woman's dress. Two weeks after his wife died in 1985 he was finally forced to leave his refuge—filthy, bearded, ragged and still terrified. To neighbors he had not seen in four decades, he could only ask, "Will I be punished?"

How do you punish a guy who'd just spent 40 years in a pigsty?

DILLINGER'S FINGERPRINTS, BACK IN CUSTODY

Since 1924, when the FBI established its Identification Division, criminals have been connected with crimes through their fingerprints. In the 1930s John Dillinger paid a renegade doctor $5,000 to remove his fingerprints with acid. He suffered agonizing pain for weeks until his fingers healed, at which point he realized his fingerprints had grown back exactly as they had been before.

A bandit operating in the 1940s, Robert James "Roscoe" Pitts is the only American criminal known to have successfully removed his fingerprints through surgery. It didn't advance his criminal career, however. Police found it even easier to identify the distinctive "blank" appearance of the prints left by the famous "man without fingerprints." Also, Pitts had had his prints erased only down to the first joint on each finger; he didn't realize that the prints left by the rest of each finger, as well as his palms, served quite adequately to identify him.

DRACO CROAKS UNDER CLOAKS

Draco was the Ancient Greek legislator who drew up the first code of law for the citizens of Athens, a code so harsh that it was said to be written in blood. Draco prescribed the death penalty for nearly every infraction. He said he considered it an appropriate punishment for minor crimes, and because he couldn't think of anything more serious, it would have to do for more serious offenses as well. Draco was popular with his fellow citizens, and in 590 B.C. a testimonial was held for him at the theater of Aegina. As he entered the arena, the crowd of his well-wishers showered him with their cloaks in a traditional show of respect. Their response was so enthusiastic that he suffocated under the cloaks.

Perhaps, in his final moments, Draco reflected on some minor peccadillo of his own and considered his demise only just.

DRIVER SMASHES RECORD

On October 15, 1966, a 75-year-old man from Frisco, Texas, set the all-time record for the most traffic offenses in the shortest amount of time. He had hitchhiked to the nearby town of McKinney to buy a car, and drove out of the used car lot at 3:50 p.m. behind the wheel of a 1953 Ford.

Four minutes later he collided with a 1952 Chevrolet driven by a local woman.

One minute later and 90 feet farther up the road, he slammed into another Chevrolet driven by a woman from out of town.

It took him only another three minutes to turn the wrong way up a one-way street and collide with a 1963 Ford.

He was beginning to develop some confidence behind the wheel, as it had been a full 14 minutes since his last collision, when he deprived a Ford Mustang of its chance to become a classic collectible.

In the space of 20 minutes, the unidentified driver had caused six accidents, committed four hit-and-run offenses and driven on the wrong side of the road four times. For his exploits he earned 10 traffic tickets plus a place in the *Guinness Book of Records* under "Worst Driver."

The motorist, who had not driven in 10 years, explained, "They don't drive like they used to."

UNSAFE AT ANY SPEED

It was generally believed that no one would ever beat the record for the quickest failure of a driving test set by Mrs. Helen Ireland of Auburn, California, in the early 1970s. She got into her car with her tester and, mistaking her gas pedal for her clutch, drove straight into the wall of the driving test center. Time required for failure: about two seconds.

A Lanarkshire, England, motor mechanic was not to be outdone. While waiting outside the test center he beeped his horn several times to summon an examiner. When an examiner did appear, it was only to inform Mr. Thomson that it was illegal to sound the horn while stationary and he had therefore failed the test. Mr. Thomson was left to ponder his remarkable feat—he had failed a driving test before he had even begun, shaving a full two seconds off the previous record.

Some fail the driving test with less speed but greater mayhem.

A 77-year-old applicant for a driver's license in Atwood, Illinois, took her place behind the wheel, the examiner beside her. She put the car in reverse and backed into a tree. Rattled, she put the car into drive and accelerated, jumping the curb and driving through the window at the test facility, killing one person and injuring four others, including the examiner.

Despite taking 273 driving lessons over a 19-year period, Betty Tudor of Exeter, England, had not been able to pass her driver's test after seven attempts. On one occasion she upset the examiner by going the wrong way around a traffic circle, but felt he took the error a bit too seriously: "I told him if it hadn't been for the cars coming in the opposite direction sounding their horns, he wouldn't have noticed anything wrong." Following another test, an examiner was admitted to a mental hospital, though Mrs. Tudor doubted that she bore any direct responsibility.

In 1981 she decided to forgo the car in favor of a moped, which requires no license.

DUELING DUNCES

The composer George Frideric Handel was challenged to a duel by Johann Mattheson. The provocation was this: Mattheson was conducting a performance of Handel's *Antony and Cleopatra* and agreed to let Handel conduct for a while. However, when Mattheson wanted to return to the podium, Handel wouldn't relinquish the baton. Mattheson (a skilled swordsman) challenged Handel (a duffer) to a duel then and there. The audience filed out to watch the two men face off in front of the opera house. With Mattheson's first jab the point of his sword got stuck in one of the thick wooden buttons on Handel's coat. The fight was then broken up, to the relief of music lovers everywhere.

Two doctors at the Charity Hospital in New Orleans disagreed over the proper treatment for an injured law student each attended to at different times of the day. Whatever treatment Dr. John Foster prescribed in the morning, Dr. Samuel Chopin would reverse in the afternoon. Somehow the patient managed to survive this erratic program. One day, when the two doctors dropped in to see him at the same time, they came to blows at his bedside and a duel was scheduled. Dr. Chopin was shot in the neck, severing his jugular vein. He eventually recovered from his wounds, but the law student was not so fortunate. Consigned to the undisturbed attentions of Dr. Foster, he soon died.

A pistol duel was fought in 1831 between Spencer Pettis, a congressman from Missouri, and U.S. Army Major Thomas Biddle over a political matter. In deference to Biddle's extreme nearsightedness, the duel was fought at a range of 5 feet. Neither participant survived.

AFTERMATH OF EARTH DAY, 1990

Earth Day went off as planned on April 22, 1990, in New York City's Central Park. Hundreds of thousands gathered to express their support for environmental programs and to display their concern for Mother Earth.

It took 50 park sanitation workers until 3 a.m. to clean up the 154.3 tons of litter the demonstrators left behind.

LET'S DO LUNCH

A band of Cambodian government troops had been in battle for over a year, the last four months of which they had not been paid, when they were visited by an army paymaster. He had come to inspect their situation but had to admit that he was unable to pay them what they were owed. The soldiers killed and ate him.

While the Ivory Coast was under colonial rule, it was represented for a time in the French senate by Victor Biaka-Boda, a former witch doctor, described by colleagues as "a small, thin, worried-looking man." In order to take a pulse reading of the body politic, Biaka-Boda set out on a fact-finding tour of his homeland in January 1950. His car broke down in the boondocks, and while his chauffeur worked on it, Biaka-Boda took a stroll into the bush, from which he never returned. In 1953 a pile of charred bones found in the area was identified as his and a court determined that he had been eaten by disgruntled constituents.

After graduating from Harvard, Michael Rockefeller, son of Governor Nelson Rockefeller and heir to the family fortune, pursued an interest in the primitive tribes of New Guinea. He traveled there extensively, and disappeared in a remote area in November 1961. He is believed to have provided lunch for some of the tribespeople that had so fascinated him.

ENGLISHMEN PURSUE PENGUINS

The idea seemed to be: While you're in purgatory anyway, why not take a side trip to Hell?

Dr. Edward A. Wilson, a member of Captain Robert Falcon Scott's ill-fated Antarctic expedition, had a particular interest in emperor penguins. He felt that much might be learned from these primitive birds about the evolutionary connection between birds and fish if some of their eggs could be brought back to England for study. Due to the creature's nesting cycle, the only time eggs could be obtained was during winter.

And so on June 22, 1911, the beginning of the Antarctic winter, Wilson, Apsley Cherry-Garrard and Lieutenant Bowers left the relative comfort of Scott's base camp on a 69-mile journey through darkness to an emperor penguin nesting site at Cape Crozier, by the foot of Mount Terror. The three men pulled 759 pounds of supplies on two wooden sledges, steering by Jupiter. Sometimes the snow made travel so difficult it took the three of them to move a single sledge, after which they had to walk back and repeat the process with the other, covering 3 miles distance for every 1 mile advance.

Temperatures rarely rose above -50°F, and at one point dipped to -77.5°F. The sweat exuded from their bodies soon caused their heavy clothing to freeze into a stiff, leaden shell. Their sleeping bags also froze into rigid sheaths, and it required an hour's effort at bedtime for Cherry-Garrard to wedge himself in, a few inches at a time, gradually thawing it with his body warmth. Once inside, his body would be racked by such prolonged bouts of violent shivering he feared his back would break. Even the fluid in the blisters on his hands froze painfully solid under his gloves. Cherry-Garrard, who was severely nearsighted, found that he could not wear his spectacles at all—they immediately iced up. More often than the others he plunged into crevasses and had to be hauled out by his rope. He ceased fearing death and began regarding it as the easy way out.

Reaching Cape Crozier at last, the trio had to cross pressure heaves of jagged ice and climb down ice cliffs to retrieve the eggs. And then they set back. As he wrote in his account of the expedition, *The Worst Journey in the World*, "The horrors of the return journey are blurred to my memory, and I know they were blurred to my body at the time...we were much weakened and callous...we slept on the march."

In 1913, back in London, Cherry-Garrard, the sole member of the trio to survive the Scott expedition, made an appointment with the British Museum to bring in the three penguin eggs. He arrived at the office of Mr. Brown, the chief custodian, who was busy chatting with another visitor. Mr. Brown took the eggs without a word and returned his attention to his guest. Cherry-Garrard waited for a considerable period until Brown turned to him, annoyed, and said, "You needn't wait."

"I should like to have a receipt for the eggs, if you please," responded the explorer.

"It's not necessary; it's all right, you needn't wait," said Brown.

When Cherry-Garrard returned to the museum later, he learned that the eggs had been misplaced.

WHO ELECTED THESE GUYS?

Ken Silverstein listed the 10 dumbest members of Congress in September 1995 for *The Progressive*. Though the list is partisan (apparently there were no dumb Democrats to be found), his evidence is fairly compelling. Some examples:

Representative Martin Hoke (R-Ohio) was wired for an interview by his local network affiliate to comment on President Clinton's 1994 State of the Union address. As the female producer who attached his mike walked away, Hoke said to the congressman standing next to him, as well as to everyone in the listening audience, "She has the *beeeeg* breasts," in a mock Mexican accent. A day later, with the furor in full bloom, Hoke expressed some relief that an escaped murderer who had gone on a killing spree in his home state might knock him out of the headlines.

Representative Don Young (R-Alaska) was present at a hearing at which Mary Tyler Moore and animal-rights activist Cleveland Amory spoke against steel jaw leg-hold traps. Amory kept punctuating his points by setting off a trap with a pencil. Deciding that some countervailing propaganda was necessary, Young placed his own hand in a trap, which snapped shut on it, and then proceeded to question a witness as if nothing unusual had happened. Later he admitted to a staffer, "I never told anyone, but it hurt like hell."

Senator Larry Pressler (R-South Dakota), leaving a meeting of the Commerce Committee, mistook a closet door for the exit. He immediately realized his mistake, but felt it would lessen his embarrassment if he waited inside until everyone else had left the room. This approach failed when all the other senators decided it would be worthwhile to wait him out. It is Pressler who is sometimes referred to as "Senator Dangerfield," for the lack of respect he commands. He once reportedly called a press conference to deny that he is dumb.

Silverstein's nomination for dumbest representative goes to Representative Jon Christensen (R-Nebraska) who, before his election, sold insurance and dealt fertilizer out of his garage, achievements he elevated in his resumé to "Insurance Marketing Director" and "Fertilizer Holding Company Executive."

During his 1994 campaign Christensen agreed to a question-and-answer session at a local high school. Afraid he'd be hit with questions he wasn't briefed on, handpicked students were given prepared questions and told to hold pens in their hands as they raised them so that the candidate would know who to call on. The choreographed session fell apart when word of the plan spread and all of the students held pens in their upraised hands. Observers wondered what question a 17-year-old could ask that would be too difficult for a congressman to answer.

Christensen once held a press conference to suggest cuts in government spending of $1.5 trillion. When a reporter informed him that $1.5 trillion represented the entire annual budget, Christensen seemed surprised and moved on to another subject.

FROM THE ANNALS OF DISORGANIZED CRIME: THE ENSULO HIT

Vinny Ensulo, a.k.a. Vinny Ba Ba, had severely strained his family ties by failing to make the $1,600 interest payment on a $1,200 loan. At about 10:30 A.M. on November 1, 1973, as he walked down Columbia Street in Brooklyn, he was jumped by James Gallo and Joe Conigliaro, soldiers in the Carlos Gambino crime family. They hustled him into a car and drove off. Gallo sat on Vinny's right, pointing a .22 pistol at his head, while Conigliaro, at the wheel, held a .38 revolver on him. Vinny was going for a ride, and he knew what that meant. After a few blocks, he made a grab for the steering wheel, causing the car to swerve and hit a parked car. Vinny lurched forward and Gallo and Conigliaro both fired their guns twice. Gallo caught two shots, in the left side and the head, and was killed. Conigliaro was hit twice, in the right shoulder and the spine, and was paralyzed. Ensulo suffered two flesh wounds and was released from the hospital that afternoon in the protective custody of the police; as the *New York Times* put it, "with a bandage on his neck and a smile on his face." His assailants remained in the trauma unit.

With the kindest of intentions no doubt, every year thereafter Vinny sent Conigliaro a gift-wrapped package of a fresh set of wheelchair batteries, with a card that read: "Keep rolling, from your best pal, Vinny Ba Ba."

ELECTRIC CHAIR: BATTERIES NOT INCLUDED

In 1890 Emperor Menelik II of Abyssinia (now Ethiopia) wished to bring to his nation some of the technological marvels that were available in industrialized societies. With a truly inspiring concern for his people's well-being, Menelik II ordered three of the brand-new electric chairs to be shipped over from New York. It was only after they arrived that he learned that they required an external power supply. Abyssinia had no electrical power. Not willing to let the technological marvels go to waste, the emperor used one of them as his throne.

Menelik II came to a strange end, and it was not due to some joker with a generator and an extension cord. Menelik is believed to be the only monarch in history to have died from eating the Bible. He had developed a habit of snacking on a few pages from the Old Testament whenever he felt the need for spiritual sustenance. Worried about his health after suffering a stroke, he went hog-wild and attempted to ingest the entire Book of Kings. He died midway, his doctors speculating that toxic chemicals in the inks had disagreed with him.

THE ELUSIVE INVESTMENTS OF W. C. FIELDS

In order to overcome a recurring nightmare of finding himself without money in a strange city, W. C. Fields opened up a bank account in every town he passed through, under such pseudonyms as Ludovic Fishpond, Colmonley Frampton-Blythe, Aristotle Hoop, Elmer Mergetroid-Haines and Figley E. Whitesides. In these accounts he squirreled away sums ranging from a few bucks to as much as $50,000. Fields neglected to keep track of them and was able to recall only 23 of the accounts before his death. He was sure he had opened at least 700, and an estimated $1,300,000 was never recovered.

FILM FLUBS FLUMMOX FANS

Sometimes, a sharp eye (or ear) and a simple grasp of logic are enough to make the filmgoer flinch. Here are some examples of Hollywood goofs mentioned in Bill Givens' *Film Flubs* series.

- In Spielberg's Academy Award-winning *The Color Purple*, Oprah Winfrey is struck with the butt of a pistol and knocked cold. As she lies on the ground the wind blows her dress up, and she modestly pushes it back down with her hand. Such self-possession, even while unconscious, helps explain how Ms. Winfrey made it to the top.
- In Cecil B. De Mille's *The Ten Commandments* (1956), Pharaoh orders the slaying of the Hebrew boys and concludes with the flourish, "So says Ramses the First." But how did he know he was the First, when Ramses the Second wasn't born until

Yul Brynner as Ramses I.

40 years later? They didn't start calling it "World War I" until World War II, after all.

- In *The Invisible Man* (1933), the main character, played by Claude Rains, has to remove his clothing in order to achieve invisibility. Near the end of the film, he strips in order to elude pursuing police. They track him by the footprints he has left in the snow—prints left by feet that are quite obviously wearing shoes.

- The plot of Orson Welles' masterpiece *Citizen Kane* revolves around a quest to discover what Charles Foster Kane meant when he breathed out his last word: "rosebud." But during that deathbed scene there doesn't appear to have been anyone around who could possibly have heard the enigmatic clue to the Kane psyche.

WORLD'S FIRST FIREPROOF THEATER

There are few more frightening situations than a fire in a crowded theater. The world's first fireproof theater, the Iroquois in Chicago, opened on December 1, 1903, and expected to do great business with its special assurance of safety. Later that month, as an orchestra played "In the Pale Moonlight," a faulty blue light intended to provide a suitable lunar ambience blew out and set fire to the scenery. The asbestos safety curtain jammed two-thirds of the way down, and the audience was asked to leave the theater, which burned to the ground before firefighters could extinguish the blaze.

WHY YOU'VE NEVER HEARD OF RENÉ FONCK

In 1924, when wealthy businessman Raymond Orteig offered a $25,000 reward to the first person to fly from New York to Paris, renowned World War I ace René Fonck seemed like a natural to claim it. Aviation pioneer Igor Sikorsky built the Frenchman an enormous three-engine biplane for the task, costing $105,000.

The plane was specially modified to carry sufficient fuel for its three thirsty engines. It carried a crew of four and had a built-in bed. It was equipped with two radios (one short-wave, one long-wave), which were massively heavy at the time. It was opulently outfitted in keeping with the pivotal role it was to play in aviation history. An interior decorator lined the inside of the cabin with mahogany panels and red Spanish leather so that it resembled "a tastefully furnished drawing room."

Sikorsky pleaded with Fonck to have the plane stress-tested, as it was 10,000 pounds beyond its engineered maximum of 28,000 pounds. Fonck ignored him, and continued to pack the plane with extra weight. Each member of the crew brought gifts for friends, and they took along a full-course dinner for six packed in vacuum containers, to be eaten upon arrival in Paris. As they were about to take off, they accepted a package of American-made croissants. (Talk about taking coals to Newcastle...)

As Fonck attempted to take off from New York's Roosevelt Field, all these tokens of assumed success weighed against him. His plane's landing gear literally bent under the strain. As Fonck gunned the engines, trying to make the 80 miles per hour speed necessary for takeoff, bits of the plane started breaking away and the rear landing wheel fell off. Unable to get off the ground, the plane tore through the fence at the end of the runway and cartwheeled into a gully, bursting into flames. Fonck and his navigator survived the crash, but his mechanic and radio operator were killed.

The accident was shown around the country on newsreels, where it attracted the attention of a young mail pilot, Charles Lindbergh, who had not previously heard of the Orteig Prize. Fonck commissioned another plane from Sikorsky for an attempt the following year, but he was beaten out by Lindbergh, who flew a stripped-down, single-engine plane across the Atlantic alone, with no radio, keeping himself awake by repeating over and over again, "There is no alternative but death and failure."

FORD DENIES IGNORANCE, FILES SUIT

Misinformed about the Ford Motor Company's policy on paying its employees for their National Guard service, the *Chicago Tribune* in 1916 denounced Ford in an angry editorial. It read, in part: "If Ford allows the rule of his shops to stand he will reveal himself not as merely an ignorant idealist but as an anarchistic enemy of the nation which protects him in his wealth. A man so ignorant as Henry Ford may not understand the fundamentals of the government under which he lives."

Ford's lawyer, Alfred Lucking, filed a $1 million libel suit, but in framing the case made a fatal error. Had he focused on the accusation that Ford was an anarchist he would have easily won, for the term had already been ruled libelous. However, Lucking characterized the entire editorial as libelous, and thus had to prove that the famed automaker was not "ignorant," a challenge that proved more difficult than one might imagine. Ford once said, "History is more or less bunk," and he gave every indication of taking that credo seriously. Lucking desperately tried to cram him with knowledge before the trial, to no avail. At the 1919 trial the *Chicago Tribune*'s lawyer, Elliot

Stevenson, cross-examined Ford mercilessly. When questioned as to the date of the American Revolution, Ford placed it in 1812. When asked to give the meaning of "chili con carne," he said it was "a large mobile army." From the transcript:

STEVENSON: Do you know of any great traitors?

FORD: No.

STEVENSON: Did you ever hear of Benedict Arnold?

FORD: I have heard the name.

STEVENSON: Who was he?

FORD: I have forgotten just who he was. A writer, I think.

The jury was not wholly unsympathetic to Ford's desire for redress. It awarded him precisely 6¢.

THE FABLED FRUGALITY OF BENJAMIN FRANKLIN

Benjamin Franklin is identified with thrift, having coined such maxims as "A penny saved is a penny earned," but he himself was a compulsive spender. While serving as ambassador to France he shipped home loads of extravagant purchases, including fine china, silverware, carpets and a harpsichord. He set up a wine cellar stocked with 1,203 bottles.While in France he spent an average of $12,000 a year, an astonishing amount of money at the time. Franklin admitted that frugality was "a virtue I never could acquire in myself."

Researchers have found that his account at Philadelphia's Bank of America was overdrawn at least three times a week.

ANOTHER STINKER ON BROADWAY: *THE FRENCH TOUCH*

When *The French Touch* opened in 1945, its press agent wanted to make the play's opening performance a memorable one. He had all the programs and usherettes liberally doused in French perfume. Fearing that the effect would not be sufficiently bold, he also had perfume blown through the theater's ventilating system. Half the audience fled the theater under the odiferous onslaught.

THE GOLDEN BANANA PEEL

Third Place: Yogi Berra

Yogi Berra, whose real name is Lawrence Peter Berra, was an all-star catcher for the New York Yankees. He later served as their manager, and also managed and coached the Mets. He is best known for his unique way with a phrase, breathing new life into tired clichés. Berra comes in last in our competition because his formulations usually make a crazy kind of sense— that's why they're so often quoted. Among his most famous are:

"It's déjà vu all over again."

At an October 24, 1963, press conference, Berra explained how he'd prepared himself for his new position as manager: "You can observe a lot by watching."

"Always go to other people's funerals; otherwise they won't go to yours."

"It's never happened in a World Series competition, and it still hasn't."

"When you reach the crossroads, take it."

Yogi had this to say about a popular restaurant: "Nobody ever goes there anymore; it's too crowded."

"If nobody wants to go to the ballpark, you can't stop them."

When asked how the mighty Yankees could have lost the 1960 World Series to the Pittsburgh Pirates, Berra explained, "We made too many wrong mistakes."

After visiting a sprawling mansion: "Wotta house. Nothin' but rooms!"

"It's very hard to predict things, especially when they're in the future."

And this final caveat from the horse's mouth: "I didn't really say everything I said."

EAT FUGU AND DIE

Since six-guns are outlawed in their country, the Japanese have come up with their own way to play Russian roulette. They eat *fugu*, the puffer or blowfish, which is deadly if not prepared to the most exacting specifications. A nerve poison called tetrodotoxin, 275 times more deadly than cyanide, is concentrated in its ovaries, intestines and liver. Despite its bland taste and gelatinous texture, raw fugu is a prized delicacy that can cost $200 a serving—obviously the danger is a large part of its appeal. Its aficionados especially enjoy the slight numbing sensation experienced in their lips, toes and fingers as trace doses of tetrodotoxin take effect. Thousands of people over the years have succumbed to improperly prepared fugu including, in 1975, Mitsugoro Bando VIII—one of Japan's most revered Kabuki actors, who had been designated a "living treasure" by the government. At the banquet celebrating his 57th birthday, his friends dared him to dine on fugu. Bando took the challenge, ordered fugu liver, gamely took a few bites and promptly dropped dead.

The lure of fugu is expressed in this bit of traditional verse:
Those who eat fugu soup are stupid.
But those who don't eat fugu soup are also stupid.

Galileo faces the Inquisition.

GALILEO GETS VATICAN OKAY

On October 30, 1992, the Catholic Church took a rare step: It admitted that it had made an error. After a 13-year investigation, Pope John Paul II made a formal statement at the Pontifical Academy of Sciences: The Church had been wrong to condemn Galileo in 1633 for saying that the earth revolved around the sun.

The discoveries Galileo made with the telescope he had built had won him renown throughout Europe and the sponsorship of powerful patrons such as the Medicis and Barberinis. But in 1632 Galileo published his *Dialogue Concerning the Two Chief World Systems* supporting the Copernican theory, which states that the sun is the center of the solar system, and debunking the popular belief that the earth is the center of the universe. For the crime of Copernicanism Galileo was summoned to the Vatican by the Inquisition. Rather than be burned at the stake, he recanted his discoveries and spent the remaining eight years of his life under house arrest.

"We today know that Galileo was right in adopting the Copernican astronomical theory," conceded Paul Cardinal Poupard, who headed the most recent investigation of the matter.

THE ENTIRELY UNNECESSARY DEATH OF PRESIDENT JAMES A. GARFIELD

When James A. Garfield, the 20th president of the United States, was shot on July 2, 1881, he probably figured that that was the worst thing that was going to happen to him all summer. Little did he know his troubles were just beginning—he was about to fall into the hands of the medical profession.

The first doctor on the scene poured half an ounce of brandy and a dram of spirits of ammonia down his throat, which Garfield promptly threw up. Garfield was then taken to the White House, where Dr. Willard Bliss, a prominent Washington doctor, was the next to torment him. In order to locate the bullet, he inserted a "Nelaton Probe" into the wound, a metal rod that probed for the point of least resistance, presumably the path opened by the slug. The Nelaton Probe, while failing to find the bullet, greatly enlarged the area of tissue damage in the chest. The probe also got stuck between the shattered fragments of Garfield's 11th rib, and was removed with great difficulty and excruciating pain. Next Bliss inserted his unwashed finger into the hole, further enlarging it and introducing infection. Other doctors called in did the same, one actually puncturing the protective outer coating of Garfield's liver with a dirty digit.

Garfield lingered on, as the American public waited anxiously for news of his condition. One citizen who decided to do more than wait was Alexander Graham Bell. He performed a few modifications to one of his telephone receivers and rigged up a crude metal detector to help locate the still-elusive slug. With his immense scientific prestige, Bell was allowed at the president's bedside to employ his device. After several passes, he was certain he had located the bullet, much deeper than had been expected. A few days later, with the president running a fever and worsening steadily, the doctors decided to cut him open at the spot Bell had indicated. Unfortunately, the bullet was not there. On September 19, 1881, Garfield died.

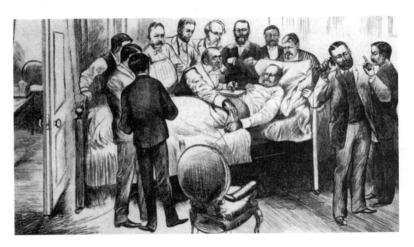

At his trial, the assassin Charles Julius Guiteau presented the sort of idiotic defense that would probably get him off today, pointing out that it was the doctors who really deserved the blame for Garfield's death. The autopsy revealed that the bullet had lodged about 4 inches from Garfield's spine and was harmlessly enveloped in a protective cyst. Had he been left alone he probably would have survived—the doctors turned a relatively harmless 3-inch hole into a 20-inch-long channel festering with infection, most of it introduced by themselves.

The argument didn't work for Guiteau. He was hanged on June 30, 1882.

ITALY'S LEAST WANTED: THE GATTI GANG

Hollywood loves terrorists—they make great villains. Unlike the run-of-the-mill street criminal, who is often embarrassingly dumb, the movie terrorist holds a master's degree in mayhem, making him a suitable foe for Stallone, Seagal or Schwarzenegger.

The Gatti Gang, a Milan-based cell of Italy's infamous Red Brigade, didn't live up to the billing. For 10 years it failed miserably to terrorize its fellow citizens.

We expect terrorists to be well armed, but members of the Gatti Gang were so unschooled in gun maintenance that all of their pistols were too rusty to fire. They tried to purchase weapons on the black market but were quickly swindled out of several thousand dollars by arms dealers who knew suckers when they saw them. The gang's naivete extended to explosives as well. They did get themselves a grenade at one time but were terrified by it. A fellow terrorist told them to "give up. You're a danger to everyone." Granted, weaponry and explosives are arcane fields of knowledge, but the Gattis were also ignorant of more mundane skills. None of them knew how to drive a car, so they generally used public transportation.

The gang finally managed to pull off a bank robbery in order to fund their subversive activities, and got away with 18,000 lira, about $25.

The gang was led by Enrico Gatti, who frequently had to cancel strategy meetings because he suffered from a chronic head cold and sinus problems. He finally gave himself up to the authorities, who probably hadn't been looking too hard for him. At his trial, he urged his 27 followers to do likewise. "Lots of our younger members want to go home and live in peace," he observed.

GOLD FEVER IN VIRGINIA

After one of the original Jamestown settlers discovered a rich vein of shiny yellow metal, gold fever struck the young colony. None other than John Smith himself lamented in his diary, "There was no thought, no discourse, no hope, and no work but to dig gold, wash gold, refine gold, and load gold." Captain Newport sent a shipload of the glittering ore back to London, along with "gladd tidings" from a land "verie Riche in gold and Copper." He was certain that the London Company, which was sponsoring the settlement, would be delighted to see its investment pay off so quickly, and that investors would flock to support more settlers. Unfortunately, assayers in London pronounced the shipment worth precisely nothing. The colonists had been mining "fool's gold," or iron pyrites.

CONNECTICUT BUYS GUNS

Seeking to imitate the success of a similar program in New York City, Connecticut initiated a gun buy-back program in February 1994. Members of the public who surrendered firearms at police stations would receive a check in the mail. The program, scheduled to run a month, had to be shut down in five days after the state ran up obligations of $489,000, nearly five times what it had expected to pay out.

The program had several flaws. It established high cash awards for firearms without regard to their actual value and it did so in a state where guns are still legally available. Entrepreneurial types immediately rushed to the nearest gun store to buy weapons for as little as $35 to $40 that could be exchanged for $100. Imported Soviet-made semiautomatic SKS rifles, available for $79.95, could be cashed in as $500 "assault rifles." One of those interviewed on his way into a police station admitted that he wanted to get rid of some cheap junk so he could put the money toward a new 9 mm semiauto. Also a mistake: Those surrendering weapons were required to fill out forms at police stations in order to receive payment, ensuring that no actual criminals would participate.

The program was quickly called to a halt with the politicians, as always, pronouncing it "a success." They did not respond to criticism that they could have gotten more guns for their money if they'd bought them directly from gun stores, cutting out the middleman.

Many of those who thought they'd made out like bandits also got burned. With the state unable to pay out as promised, it had to fall back on vouchers offered by area businesses. Many who'd turned in guns hoping to put the money toward a new 9 mm instead got tickets to see the perenially losing Hartford Whalers hockey team.

CRIMES OF THE HANDICAPPED

David Worrell, 25, got a 12-year suspended sentence for his attempted bank robbery in London. The sentence was light because the judge did not feel Worrell posed a significant threat to society. Worrell, a blind man, had tried to hold up a bank using his cane as a weapon. When he heard the police sirens outside, he panicked and ran smack into a door.

Jeffrey Meruked, 29, was an armed robber who didn't discourage easily. In 1967 he was captured by police in Buffalo, New York, during his getaway attempt after a convenience store robbery, when he fell from his wheelchair, which his accomplice was pushing too fast. Meruked had lost the use of his legs after he was shot during a robbery attempt earlier that year.

In 1990 a blind man was arrested after a bank robbery in which he handed a threatening note to the teller and, after receiving $105, asked for her help in leaving the building.

Two men, one aged 76 and the other 77, fired a total of 12 pistol shots at each other at point-blank range in a Cleveland apartment in 1984. Neither was injured. Police speculate that the men escaped unscathed from the furious firefight because one had glaucoma and the other had to prop himself up with his cane before each shot.

A 350-pound armed robber got the receipts of a Long Island, New York, jeweler, but while making his escape fell to the floor and was unable to get up before the police arrived.

THE UNEVENTFUL TERM OF PRESIDENT WILLIAM HENRY HARRISON

Early into his presidency Bill Clinton mused that he hadn't accomplished as much as he'd hoped, but on the other hand, at the same point in his first term William Henry Harrison was already dead.

William Henry Harrison was elected president in 1840, and was determined to deliver a memorable inaugural speech. The inauguration was on the coldest day of the year, and Harrison delivered his two-hour speech in a freezing downpour, refusing to wear a hat, scarf or coat. In one prophetic line, he said he would not run for a second term. After the speech, he drank and danced at three inaugural balls until the wee hours.

Harrison had had a cold at the time of his inauguration, which soon developed into pneumonia. Exactly one month after he assumed the presidency, Harrison was dead.

GARY HART ISSUES A CHALLENGE TO THE PRESS

In 1987 Senator Gary Hart was the front-runner for the 1988 Democratic presidential nomination but was dogged by rumors of reckless womanizing. Proclaimimg the soundness of his marriage, he issued a challenge to a reporter from the *New York Times*: "Follow me around. I don't care. I'm serious. If anybody wants to put a tail on me, go ahead. They'd be very bored."

What reporter could resist a challenge like that? Days later the *Miami Herald* broke the story that Donna Rice, a stunning blond saleswoman and part-time actress and model, had spent the night at Hart's Washington townhouse. A few weeks later the *National Enquirer* published a photo of Rice sitting on Hart's lap on a chartered yacht called the *Monkey Business*.

Comedians had a field day: "Reagan's slogan might be 'Win one for the Gipper,' but Hart would ask us to 'Win one for the zipper.'" Or, "His new campaign manager would be Dr. Ruth, his pollsters Masters and Johnson." Johnny Carson suggested that Hart campaign in a Santa Claus suit, so he would have a ready excuse the next time he was photographed with a girl on his lap. Letterman said that among Hart's Top 10 Christmas wishes was "That people start referring to sleazy womanizing as 'Kennedyesque.'"

Though his wife stood by him, Hart's fund-raising dried up and his press conferences were reduced to probing questions about his sex life. He had to drop out of the race in May 1987.

The *New York Daily News* published a letter from a man who contemplated the matter and reached his own determination. He wrote:

"After seeing Donna Rice's picture in the *Daily News*, I can say truthfully that I would rather spend one night with Donna Rice than be president of the United States. This country stinks anyway. I gotta hand it to you, Gary, you made the right choice."

Gary Hart continues to consider a return to politics. Donna Rice is now married and an antiporn crusader.

PECULIAR HEADLINES

HERE'S HOW YOU CAN LICK DOBERMAN'S LEG SORES
—Reading (Pennsylvania) *Eagle*

SKELETON TIED TO MISSING DIPLOMAT
—Philadelphia *Evening Bulletin*

TWO CONVICTS EVADE NOOSE; JURY HUNG
—Oakland *Tribune*

JUVENILE COURT TO TRY SHOOTING DEFENDANT
—Deseret *News*

GLASS EYE NO HELP IN IDENTIFYING CORPSE
—Deseret *News*

HOSPITALS ARE SUED BY 7 FOOT DOCTORS
—Providence (Rhode Island) *Journal*

DOCTOR TESTIFIES IN HORSE SUIT
—Waterbury (Connecticut) *Republican*

UTAH GIRL DOES WELL IN DOG SHOWS
—Salt Lake *Tribune*

BRITISH LEFT WAFFLES ON FALKLANDS
—*The Guardian*

CENTER TO AID VETERANS BEING RESURRECTED
—The Louisville (Kentucky) *Times*

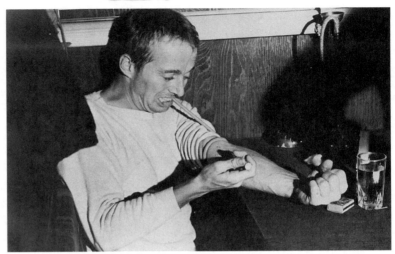

CURE FOUND FOR MORPHINE ADDICTION!

Morphine was first isolated from the opium poppy early in the nineteenth century and used as a highly effective painkiller. Its addictive properties caused concern though, and in 1898 Dr. Heinrich Dreser, who headed the drug research laboratory at Germany's Bayer Company, was pleased to announce that he had developed a nonaddictive substitute. It was diacetylmorphine, which the company marketed under the name heroin. Heroin is a morphine derivative that is four to eight times as effective as a painkiller; unfortunately, it is also far more addictive. Until that was discovered, heroin was used in cough syrups and pain remedies, and was prescribed by doctors for headaches, menstrual cramps and even as a method of curing morphine addiction.

It was 12 years before doctors realized the seriousness of the heroin problem, and in 1924 its manufacture was banned in the United States. Unfortunately, by that time there were so many desperate addicts that organized crime was happy to service their needs.

THE MAN WHO SHOT WILD BILL HICKOK

A few days before he died, Wild West legend Wild Bill Hickok had a premonition. He remarked to a friend, "I feel my days are numbered. Somebody is going to kill me. I don't know who, or why."

On the fateful day in August 1876, as he played poker in a Deadwood Gulch saloon, Hickok made a fatal error. He did not take his habitual precaution of sitting with his back to a wall. Jack McCall, a drifter who fancied himself a gunslinger, walked up behind Hickok and shot him dead.

McCall ran out of the saloon and jumped on the nearest horse. By killing Wild Bill he'd made his name, but he hadn't yet made his getaway. And he wouldn't—he'd chosen a horse with a loose saddle. He flipped over the side of the horse, was collared by the irate citizens of Deadwood and later strung up.

HOW HITLER SPENT D DAY

Hitler, in his insanity, made so many errors in World War II that it's almost fair to say that "we couldn't have won it without him." Entire books have been written about his blunders, but one incident stands out.

By early 1944 the Germans knew that invasion was imminent—the only question was where in France the Allies would strike. Generals von Rundstedt and Rommel were entrusted with the defense of occupied France. A powerful German armored force was stationed inland in reserve, available to be brought to bear against the Allies wherever they landed.

When the invasion began with parachute landings before dawn on June 6, General von Rundstedt took a chance and ordered two Panzer divisions to speed toward the Normandy beachhead. As the hours passed and the scope of the assault grew apparent, von Rundstedt felt vindicated. This was clearly no diversion—it was the invasion they had been anticipating.

Just as von Rundstedt considered the German defense well in hand, he was shocked to receive a call from Hitler's headquarters, excoriating him for having ordered the armed forces into action without direct authorization from the Führer. The two divisions had been ordered to halt their advance until Hitler gave the go-ahead. As the day wore on and the Allies' beachhead grew larger and stronger, the divisions still did not arrive. Von Rundstedt repeatedly telephoned headquarters to find out what Hitler had decided. The staff could not tell him. As was his habit, Hitler was sleeping until the middle of the afternoon, and no one dared wake him. By the time Hitler arose and agreed to the deployment of the Panzer divisions, it was too late.

HOLLYWOOD RATED "X"... FOR WRONG

Sometimes too much knowledge can spoil your enjoyment of Hollywood entertainment.

In *Gone with the Wind*, Civil War buffs have noted that if you time Melanie's pregnancy against the dates of the battles mentioned, you wind up with a pregnancy of 21 months. Author Margaret Mitchell, when told of the error, explained that southerners always do things at a slower pace than Yankees.

Krakatoa, East of Java, annoyed those conversant with geog-

raphy. The island of Krakatoa lies west of Java, not east.

No one who has seen it will ever forget Janet Leigh's death scene in *Psycho*, ending with the extreme closeup of her eye. It was spoiled for medical experts by the fact that the actress's pupil was contracted to a pinpoint, a normal reaction to the bright lights on the set. They noted that when people die their muscles relax, causing their pupils to dilate.

In *The Wizard of Oz*, after the Scarecrow gets his diploma from the Wizard, he displays his newfound brainpower by spouting a geometric theorem: "The sum of the square roots of any two sides of an isosceles triangle is equal to the square root of the remaining side." The average moviegoer may have been impressed, but mathematicians were baffled; what the Scarecrow said made no sense whatsoever.

Sometimes the mere ability to count lets you know that something is amiss.

In the climactic shootout in *Butch Cassidy and the Sundance Kid*, Robert Redford loads up his two six-shooters and then

manages to get 17 shots out of them. You can get away with anything when you're that good-looking.

During filming of the lengthy car chase in *Bullit*, somebody on the crew lost track of a few details. Steve McQueen's Dodge Charger loses three hubcaps in the course of the chase, but when he crashes at the chase's end three more fly off.

THE REAL HORATIO ALGER STORY

Horatio Alger was the most popular American writer in the latter half of the nineteenth century, writing 135 books and creating his own distinct literary genre. The "Horatio Alger story" always focuses on a poor boy who, through a combination of luck, pluck, perseverance and prudence, makes a great financial success of himself. Those who make it from rags to riches are inevitably compared to Horatio Alger.

Unfortunately, though Alger achieved great wealth in his lifetime, his was no Horatio Alger story. He was a compulsive spender and died penniless.

NO ESCAPE FOR HOUDINI

Harry Houdini remains history's most renowned magician and escape artist. He not only escaped from manacles and straitjackets, but seemed to cheat death with such feats as diving into the Seine River wearing handcuffs, or being soldered into a metal coffin that was then submerged underwater for an hour and a half.

But death had the last laugh, because Houdini met his end through a foolish blunder. He had allowed some fans into his dressing room after a show at the Princess Theater in Montreal on October 22, 1926. He was relaxing on his couch, reading his mail, when one of the young men, J. Gordon Whitehead, asked if it was true that Houdini could take punches to his midsection without injury. Distracted by his mail, Houdini answered in the affirmative and gave him permission to try. Whitehead punched him immediately, very hard, and followed up with three quick jabs. Houdini, who had not tensed his muscles in preparation for the attack, soon felt a burning pain. Eight days later, on Halloween, he died of peritonitis from a ruptured appendix.

HOWARD HUGHES' FAVORITE FLAVOR

In the last 15 years of his life, billionaire Howard Hughes withdrew entirely from the outside world. He would rent an entire floor of a luxury hotel where, protected and served by his "Mormon Mafia," he lay in bed in a darkened room for weeks at a time, never bathing or brushing his teeth, watching movies over and over again and following strange, obsessive diets.

Since Hughes would often lose interest in food, causing his weight to plummet alarmingly, aides catered to his odd whims in order to get him to eat anything at all. There were periods when he would eat nothing but candy bars and nuts, washed down with milk; during another period he ate only chicken soup from cans. At other times it was ice cream. While ensconced in his suite at the Desert Inn in Las Vegas, Hughes tried each of Baskin Robbins' 31 flavors. He decided he liked "banana nut" the best, and after that he ate two scoops of it with every meal. His staff always kept plenty on hand.

One day, when an aide went to replenish the supply, he got alarming news—the flavor had been discontinued. Everyone went into a panic. They had only enough banana nut for a few more servings, and no one looked forward to telling Howard Hughes that he couldn't have what he wanted. Desperate, they contacted the Baskin Robbins plant in Los Angeles. The manufacturer agreed to make up a special batch; the only catch was that they'd have to order 350 gallons. The aides agreed, and drove all night to to bring back the ice cream. The food storage freezers in the Desert Inn's kitchen had to be completely rearranged to accommodate it. The staff was relieved—they had gotten down to the last few scoops of their old supply, but now they had enough for a lifetime.

The next day, after Hughes dined on his habitual two scoops of banana nut, he told his aide, "That's great ice cream, but it's time for a change. From now on I want French vanilla."

THE SPREADING IGNORANCE EPIDEMIC

Responding to a 1988 ABC-TV poll that tested high school seniors on their knowledge of world events, a girl said that the Holocaust was "that Jewish holiday last week, right?" Another student thought the Ayatollah was a Soviet gymnast. One student who was asked what Chernobyl was guessed that it was Cher's full name.

The following print ad for a popular brand of vodka was dropped after a short run:

"I THOUGHT THE KAMASUTRA WAS AN INDIAN RESTAURANT UNTIL I DISCOVERED SMIRNOFF."

The ad had to be dropped when it was discovered that most people surveyed had no idea that the Kamasutra was *not* an Indian restaurant.

After Mickey Mantle received his liver transplant, his doctor gave a press conference at which he mentioned that the same donor who had provided Mantle with his liver had provided seven other vital organs to patients who needed them.

One of the reporters present asked the doctor if it would be possible to speak with that extraordinarily generous donor.

A reporter for the *New York Times* talked to college students who admit they don't read books. One sophomore, who acknowledged that she had not read a book since starting college, attributed it to a newly recognized lifestyle.

"It's called 'alliteracy,'" she declared, showing the reporter a magazine article about the phenomenon. "It means that students know how to read and write, but just don't have the interest."

The syndrome was compared to asexuality, in which people have the ability to perform sexually but prefer not to.

"It may cause problems for us later on," another student admitted, "but we try not to dwindle on it."

Senator Roman Hruska (R-Nebraska) defended Nixon's controversial nomination of Harold G. Carswell to the Supreme Court, saying, "Even if he were mediocre, there are a lot of mediocre judges and people and lawyers. They are entitled to a little representation, aren't they, and a little chance?"

POSSIBLE CAUSES OF THE IGNORANCE EPIDEMIC

While running for governor of Louisiana, Edwin W. Edwards invited a television audience to write to his campaign head-quarters for his "comprehensive ten-point plan to improve education." Those who did were sent a plan containing exactly nine points.

In the early 1990s, the Texas Board of Education ordered $20 million worth of new history books from such reputable publishers as Houghton Mifflin; Holt, Rinehart & Winston; Prentice-Hall; and Scott Foresman & Co. After noticing some obvious historical inaccuracies in the four texts, the board submitted them to experts who identified nearly 3,700 additional errors. Among them were the claims that Robert Kennedy and Martin Luther King, Jr., were assassinated during the Nixon Administration, that George Bush was elected president in 1989 and that the United States won the Korean War by dropping "the bomb."

Eighth graders in New Jersey may have been perplexed by an achievement exam administered statewide in the spring of 1992. The multiple-choice exam, which cost $1.1 million to prepare and was taken by 70,000 students, included a math question for which there was no correct answer, another for which there were two correct answers, a map that mistakenly identified Colorado as Utah and questions pertaining to reading passages that had not been included on the test form.

Teachers in St. Joseph, Missouri, mounted a letter-writing campaign to Governor John Ashcroft appealing for more state aid for education. Unfortunately, the teachers' letters were replete with spelling and grammatical errors. Some used "their" when they meant "they're," others addressed the governor as "govenor," and one pleaded: "Don't leave us with a legacy of mediocricy in education."

In 1969 this headline appeared in the *New York Post*: "Allen's Goal: End Illitercy in U.S."

The *New York Times* once ran an article on the education crisis under the headline "The Return to Fundementals in the Nation's Schools."

The class of 1990 at the United States Naval Academy received diplomas that identified them as graduates of the "Navel Academy." The printing error was discovered too late to be corrected in time for the commencement ceremony.

A close examination of the wildly successful board game Trivial Pursuit, which tests players' knowledge of obscure information, revealed that many of the facts on the cards are inaccurate. The creators dismissed the criticism. "This is a game we're talking about, not the Pentagon," said a company spokesman.

PLEASE DESCRIBE THE ACCIDENT IN YOUR OWN WORDS...

Motorists involved in traffic accidents are required to describe the circumstances for their insurance companies. Some of the descriptions reflect the drivers' confusion at the time of the accidents, and others the understandable desire of the drivers to distance themselves from responsibility. The following explanations, taken from actual insurance company forms, were published in the *Toronto Sun* on July 26, 1977.

- Coming home I drove into the wrong house and collided with a tree I don't have.
- The other car collided with mine without giving warning of its intentions.
- The pedestrian had no idea which way to run, so I ran over him.
- I collided with a stationary truck coming the other way.
- A truck backed through my windshield into my wife's face.
- A pedestrian hit me and went under my car.
- The guy was all over the road; I had to swerve a number of times before I hit him.
- In my attempt to kill a fly, I drove into a telephone pole.
- I pulled away from the side of the road, glanced at my mother-in-law and headed over the embankment.

- I had been driving for 40 years when I fell asleep at the wheel and had an accident.
- To avoid hitting the bumper of the car in front, I hit the pedestrian.
- My car was legally parked as it backed into the other vehicle.
- An invisible car came out of nowhere, struck my car and vanished.
- I told the police that I was not injured but on removing my hat I found that I had a fractured skull.
- I thought my window was down but I found out that it was up when I put my head through it.
- I saw a slow-moving, sad-faced old man as he bounced off the roof of my car.
- The indirect cause of the accident was a little guy in a small car with a big mouth.
- I was thrown from the car as it left the road. I was later found in a ditch by some stray cows.
- The telephone pole was approaching. I was attempting to swerve out of its way when it struck the front end.
- I was on my way to the doctor with rear-end trouble when my universal joint gave way causing me to have an accident.
- I was unable to stop in time and my car crashed into the other

vehicle. The driver and passengers then left immediately for a vacation with injuries.

THEY CALL IT "INTELLIGENCE"

Though they call it "intelligence," those who spy for their countries are not always the brightest.

Two German spies set up shop in Portsmouth, England, during World War I, posing as cigar importers. They sent coded cables back to their superiors, using quantities of cigars to communicate information about British naval activity. British suspicions were aroused by the size of their cigar orders—48,000 in 10 days—more than the citizens of Portsmouth could smoke in a decade. The spies were arrested.

The English money system is confusing at best, and it caused at least one World War II German infiltrator who was trying to pass as an Englishman to give himself away. Asking the price of a railway ticket at a station, he was told "ten and six." The spy obediently handed over 10 pounds and six shillings to the clerk. The suspicious clerk summoned a guard. Any proper Englishman knows that "ten and six" means 10 shillings and six pence. The spy had paid more than 18 times the going rate without flinching.

In 1945 Soviet diplomats bestowed an impressive gift upon U.S. Ambassador W. Averell Harriman. It was a facsimile of the Great Seal of the United States, hand-carved from wood. Harriman gave it an honored place in his study. Though an educated man, Harriman was evidently unfamiliar with the story of the Trojan Horse. The present he had hung on his wall contained a listening device with which the Russians could monitor conversations in his private study. The bug was not discovered until 1952.

A former FBI agent writing in the *Nation* magazine claimed that the Bureau had 1,500 informants in the American Communist Party, or one agent for every 5.7 regular members. The informants all dutifully paid their membership fees, making the U.S. government the largest financial supporter of the American Communist Party after the USSR itself.

British intelligence official Sir Peregrine Henniker-Heaton disappeared after telling his wife he was going for a stroll on October 5, 1971, prompting fears that he had been assassinated by foreign agents. A search was launched that failed to turn up any leads as to his whereabouts for three years. In June 1974 his decomposed body was found in a locked room of his own house, where it had been all the time. Henniker-Heaton had committed suicide. Scotland Yard had failed to look for him at home.

FBI agents launched an investigation as to how U.S. military secrets got inside a piñata bought by an unidentified woman at a Sears store in Rochester, New York. The papier-mâché piñata, which should have been empty, was sold for $6.99. The woman who bought it notified the FBI when she discovered that it contained classified documents.

In 1995 the Defense Intelligence Agency admitted that in the past 10 years it had spent $20 million on psychics. Among the tidbits of information provided was that General Dozier, kidnapped by Italy's Red Brigade terrorists, was being held in a

Defense intelligence agency employs psychics.

stone house with a red roof, a clue that narrowed the search down to about 75% of the buildings in Italy. Senator Inouye (D-Hawaii) and Senator Byrd (D-West Virginia) were particularly enamored of the program, which has only recently been shut down due to lack of results. Among other things, the psychics failed to predict the collapse of the Soviet Union.

IT'S THE THOUGHT THAT COUNTS

A United States plane dropping relief supplies to Rwandan refugees during the 1994 emergency missed its drop zone. Seventeen tons of corned beef, flour and other foods were scattered on the refugees, injuring several, as well as nearly destroying a UN helicopter and a school.

The same problem arose after the Persian Gulf War, when pallets of food and supplies were air-dropped to Kurdish refugees on the border of Turkey and Iraq. At least eight died, crushed by aid supplies.

To add insult to injury, included in the food packages were pork sausages, luncheon meats and bacon burgers, which the International Red Cross had explicitly asked not be sent to the devoutly Islamic Kurds.

After a spate of terrorist bombings, when Italian police found an unattended car parked illegally at Rome's Leonardo da Vinci Airport, they suspected it might contain a bomb. They had already blown open the car's doors with explosives when the driver of the car returned.

The car, a $100,000 armor-plated Mercedes-Benz 500, belonged to U.S. General James Brown, commander of NATO air forces in southern Europe. The car had been left while the driver helped him into the terminal with his bags. It did not contain a bomb.

In 1991 the Sony Corporation announced it would present famed ragtime pianist Eubie Blake with its first Legendary Innovator Award, at a special ceremony to be held in his honor. In its invitation to Blake, Sony expressed its hope that he would attend, and noted that his presence would be a tremendously "uplifting experience." Indeed it would have been; Blake had been dead for eight years.

The antidrug advertising campaign that announces "This is your brain on drugs" while showing an egg frying in a pan has had unexpected results. According to an article in *Advertising Age*, impressionable youngsters all over the country have been refusing to eat fried eggs, believing that they contain drugs that will do bad things to their brains.

The British army was called out during the London firefighters' strike of the late 1970s to provide fire protection and perform emergency rescue tasks. One of the calls they received was from an elderly woman whose cat was stuck up a tree. Responding in time-honored fashion, the troops drove a hook-and-ladder truck to the scene and rescued the cat. Pleased with a job well done, and charmed by the elderly woman's effusive gratitude, the men accepted her invitation to tea. At last the heroes bade their farewells and got back aboard their truck to return to the station. While pulling away from the curb, they ran over the cat.

An Emergency Medical Service crew in New York rushed to an emergency room with what it took to be an abandoned fetus. It turned out to be an abandoned bag of spaghetti.

IRAN UNEARTHS ANCIENT RELIC

In what for a time appeared to be one of the most important finds of the century, paleontologists in 1930 unearthed what appeared to be the skeletal remains of a dinosaur near Teheran, Iran (then called Persia). A scientific team flew in from Madrid in order to help identify the find. It reported that the parts that had been discovered belonged to a derelict hay-making machine that had evidently been buried in a landslide a few decades earlier.

IVORY SNOW GIRL COMES CLEAN

In 1970 Procter & Gamble found a model, Marilyn Briggs, with just the right quality of purity and innocence it was looking for. Briggs, wrapped in a white terry cloth robe, gazed adoringly at her baby on the cover of the Ivory Snow box.

Three years later Procter & Gamble got a shock when it discovered that the demure mom on their soap box was none other than Marilyn Chambers, better known by millions without her bathrobe. She was the star of the hard-core pornographic hit *Behind the Green Door*. Chambers had a lucrative porn career for years afterward, billing herself as "The Ivory Snow Girl."

REMEMBER IWO JIMA

Iwo Jima was probably the hardest-fought battle of World War II. It lasted for 26 days, cost the lives of 5,563 marines and wounded 17,343. Taking the island was considered essential to victory against the Japanese. The statue at the Arlington National Cemetery of U.S. Marines raising the flag atop Mt. Suribachi is one of America's most sacred war memorials, so it is understandable that, a few years back, Congressman Charles Joelson (D-New Jersey) took to the floor of the House to express his astonishment that the souvenir statuettes sold at the memorial were all "Made in Japan."

JOHNSON, LYNDON BAINES; THE WIT AND WISDOM OF

Lyndon Johnson was a compulsive gift giver who would always pull something out of his pocket to give a guest, usually a pocketknife or cigarette lighter emblazoned with his name. His son-in-law Patrick Nugent recalled that he'd say, "Here, I want you to keep this as a memento of your visit to the ranch, but for God's sake don't embarrass me by leaving it in a whorehouse someplace."

On a 1966 trip to Asia he brought along "a planeload" of plastic busts of himself, which he handed out as special gifts. Later, when Pope Paul VI gave him a valuable fourteenth-century painting as a Christmas gift, Johnson gave him one of the busts in return.

During the urban riots that convulsed many of America's cities during the 1960s, Johnson observed that "killing, rioting and looting are contrary to the best traditions of this country."

Johnson's vice president, Hubert Humphrey, had this to say about his boss: "No sane person in the country likes the war in Vietnam, and neither does President Johnson."

CAPTAIN KIDD'S UNFORTUNATE ADVENTURE

Captain Kidd is regarded as one of history's most bloodthirsty pirates, but the legend bears little relation to the truth. Until events turned against him, Kidd was regarded as a devoted husband and father, a successful merchant and property owner, a naval hero and a "well-beloved agent" of King William III of England. In 1695 Kidd was put in command of the *Adventure*

Galley, a privateer with a commission to plunder the ships of England's enemy, France. Kidd knew that the line between legally sanctioned privateering and piracy was a fine one, and he was careful to hire a crew that knew the difference. In London, he took on 70 men, nearly all of whom were married with families in New England. Unfortunately, as it turned out, the effort didn't save him.

As the *Adventure Galley* sailed down the Thames, it passed a yacht of the Royal Navy. It was customary under such circumstances to fire a salute, but Kidd failed to do so. To remind him to show respect, the yacht fired a shot of its own. The crew of the *Adventure Galley*, all up in the yard arms handling sail, chose to respond in a most inappropriate fashion. Turning their backs on the naval yacht, they bent over and slapped their backsides, a seventeenth century version of mooning. Shortly thereafter, a man-of-war brought a press-gang to board Kidd's vessel, and nearly all of his handpicked men were forcibly taken off for service in the navy and replaced with naval rejects. Upon his arrival in New York, Kidd had to fill out his crew with the dregs of the docks, most of whom had already developed a taste for piracy. Once on the high seas these men pushed Kidd to be more open-minded in his choice of targets than was legally advisable.

Kidd's death on the gallows was largely due to that moon over the Thames.

KKK RAISES STANDARDS FOR MEMBERSHIP

In 1989 the Mississippi Christian Knights of the Ku Klux Klan were forced to unseat Jordan Gollub as their Grand Dragon after they discovered that he was Jewish. Mr. Gollub, who was born of Jewish parents in Philadelphia, had been defrocked in Virginia as Grand Dragon of its chapter of the racist and anti-Semitic organization four years previously.

Meeting intolerance at every turn, Gollub pledged to start his own chapter.

KKK PROTECTS ITS SACRED TEXT

In 1916 Joseph Simmons, Imperial Wizard of the Ku Klux Klan, issued an "Imperial Decree" intended to protect the absolute secrecy of the Klan's sacred text:

"The *Kloran* is *the* book of the Invisible Empire and is therefore a sacred book with our citizens, and its contents must be rigidly safeguarded. The book or any part of it must not be kept or carried where any person of the 'alien' world may chance to become acquainted with its sacred contents as such. *In warning:* a penalty sufficient will speedily be enforced for disregarding the decree in the profanation of the *Kloran*."

Shortly thereafter, Simmons decided that any book as important as the *Kloran* must be copyrighted, so he sent two copies along with a registration fee to the Register of Copyrights at the Library of Congress, where it can be checked out by anyone who wants a look at it.

KMARTO WINE, FOR THE TRUE KONNISEWER

When you think of wine, you think of field hands picking ripe grapes on sunny hillsides, rows of wooden casks in the cool cellar of a stately chateau and purse-lipped connoisseurs savoring the bouquet of a rare vintage. You don't think of K-Mart. Nevertheless, in the mid-1980s, K-Mart stores in the Gainesville, Florida, area, began selling their own house brand, "Kmarto," bottled by the St. John's Beverage Company in St. Augustine, and available in both red and white. Customers were not completely immune to the Kmarto allure—many knew a perfect gag gift when they saw one, especially after its initial cost of $1.97 was marked down to 99¢ for clearance. Gary Kirkland wrote about Kmarto for the *Gainesville Sun* and received a number of calls from area residents who still treasure their vintage bottles of the stuff. Oddly, it didn't seem to have occurred to any of them to actually drink it—it was kept solely for its shock value. Many feel it broadens the scope of a well-stocked wine rack. One family uses it as the centerpiece for all important family photos—weddings, reunions, birthdays, etc.—to give events that special élan. In another family it has become traditional, whenever an expensive wine is served, to acknowledge that, *of course*, it cannot compare with the debonair-yet-somehow-impudent Kmarto.

WHO HIT ME?

In a heavyweight bout at Long Island's Garden Arena, before a crowd of 1,500, Henry Wallitsch made boxing history on September 12, 1959. Wallitsch was fighting a grudge match against Bartolo Soni of the Dominican Republic, whom he had lost to on a split decision six weeks earlier.

The scheduled 10-round match was in its third round, with few solid blows having been landed. After breaking free of a clinch, Wallitsch wound up and threw a wild haymaker, and hit nothing but air. He lost his balance, pitched headfirst through the ropes, slammed his chin on the ring's apron and was knocked cold.

Though Soni got credit in the record books for the third-round kayo, he must have known he didn't really deserve it. After all, it was Wallitsch who had scored the knockout blow.

OOPS! SPECIAL SECTION: THE HAPLESS HISTORY OF *REALLY* BIG AIRPLANES

The Bible says, "Pride goeth before destruction, and a haughty spirit before a fall," and never more so than when one aspires to build The World's Biggest Airplane. The history of aviation is littered with the wrecked dreams of those who sought that honor.

IN THE TRADITION OF ITALIAN GRAND OPERA: THE CA-90 TRANSAEREO

In 1921 Italy's Count Caproni gave the locals something to talk about when he took his Ca-90 "Transaereo" out for a spin on Lake Maggiore. The Transaereo was a remarkable contraption, looking less like an aircraft than something that should have been sailing with the Spanish Armada. The fuselage was a 77-foot houseboat, and on top of it—at front, back and center—were mounted three triplane wings, for a total of nine. It had eight Liberty engines, four at the front pulling and four at the rear pushing.

All evidence to the contrary, the Transaereo was not the creation of a complete fool. Caproni had had considerable success designing large bombers for the Italian air force in World War I. The Transaereo was intended to carry 100 passengers across the Atlantic.

For its maiden flight, Caproni approximated the weight of the passengers with ballast. The test pilot took the Transaereo up to 60 feet above Lake Maggiore, at which point the ballast shifted and the plane headed nose-down into the drink. The pilot survived the crash.

A photo exists of the wreckage, with boats surrounding the floating passenger cabin, the broken wings piled in heaps around it. If you look closely at the face of one of the boatmen, you can see that he is laughing.

JUST PLANE SLOW: THE DORNIER GIANT FLYING BOAT

Claude Dornier's Do-X ("X" for the "unknown quantity") seaplane, completed in 1929, was intended for transatlantic passenger service. It was luxuriously appointed, with little sleeping cabins opening onto a carpeted hallway; a kitchen; and rooms for dining, smoking and recreation.

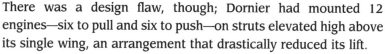

There was a design flaw, though; Dornier had mounted 12 engines—six to pull and six to push—on struts elevated high above its single wing, an arrangement that drastically reduced its lift.

Still, Dornier was determined to make a transatlantic flight. The Do-X set off in November 1930 with a crew of 19 and a load of mail. It limped from one European port to another, with a month off in Lisbon to repair fire damage, then to the Canary Islands, where, trying to take off in choppy seas, its hull was damaged so badly that it had to return to port for three months' worth of repairs. It made the 1,400-mile leap to Brazil only by leaving half the crew and all extra clothing behind, and by flying just 20 feet above the waves to get "ground effect," the extra lift achieved when air is cushioned between wings and the sea. The Do-X lingered a while in Brazil, at last reaching New York on August 27, 1931, having made the 12,000-mile trip in 10 months. That works out to 1.6 miles per hour.

There was no interest expressed in Do-X transatlantic passenger service. The giant plane ended up in a Berlin air museum, where Allied bombers put it out of its misery in World War II.

TRIUMPH AND TRAGEDY OF THE MAXIM GORKY

In the early 1930s the Union of Soviet Writers and Editors held a fund-raising drive to construct a giant aircraft to be named the "Maxim Gorky," to commemorate the upcoming 40th anniversary of the commencement of the great Russian author's literary career. Six million rubles were raised, and when the ANT-20 was completed in 1934 it was the biggest airplane on earth. It could carry a crew of 20 and up to 80 passengers in distinctly nonsocialistic comfort: There was a bar and a buffet, a 16-line telephone exchange, a laundry, a pharmacy, toilets and cabins for 12. It had a theater in the rear fuselage featuring propaganda films, and a newspaper office complete with printing press built into its (where else?) left wing. Loudspeakers broadcast the communist message to the cities over which it flew, as well as to astonished peasants working in rural areas.

A year after it was completed the *Maxim Gorky* was flying over Moscow with a small fighter plane alongside it to provide scale. Unfortunately, the fighter pilot, Comrade Blagin, decided to show off with a few aeronautical stunts. While demonstrating a barrel roll he crashed on top of the *Maxim Gorky*. The giant plane came apart in the air, spewing out passengers, telephones, laundry appliances, the film projector and the printing press.

The Stalinist press directed public outrage at the late fighter pilot whose desire to show off had caused the accident. A new word, "blaginism," was coined to describe selfish exhibitionism and the lack of proper socialistic restraint.

HUGHES' ALBATROSS: THE SPRUCE GOOSE

At the outset of World War II German submarines posed a grave peril, sinking as much as 50% of Allied shipping. A solution that occurred to shipping tycoon Henry J. Kaiser was to design airplanes large enough to do the work of cargo ships. In 1942 he formed a partnership with Howard Hughes to build a giant flying boat, the Hercules HK-1. The seaplane they envisioned would be capable of carrying 60 tons of cargo, the equivalent of 750 battle-equipped troops or a Sherman tank. They got an $18 million appropriation to build three prototypes, and promised that they would eventually be able to produce 500 flying boats a year.

During the war aluminum was restricted as a "strategic material," so Hughes recommended that they build the HK-1 from resin-impregnated wood. (Though it was dubbed the "Spruce Goose"—a name that Hughes detested—the flying boat had no spruce in it. It was made almost entirely from birch.) They had promised to deliver the first three planes within 10 months, but Hughes' growing obsessiveness began to slow the project down. He had to approve every nut and bolt before it could be installed, and sent engineers through forests all over the U.S. and Canada searching out specific trees for specific parts of the plane.

As the war wound on, the HK-1 was no longer needed and government funds were cut off. Kaiser dropped out of the partnership, but Hughes kept building, sinking $7 million of his own money into it. It was finally completed nearly a year after the war ended in 1946. The *Spruce Goose* was the largest plane ever built, with a wingspan half again as wide as that of a Boeing 747, but it was already obsolete, ridiculed as a white elephant.

On November 2, 1947, Hughes took the *Spruce Goose* out for taxi trials in Long Beach Harbor. As if to prove wrong those who said it could never fly, he revved up the eight Pratt & Whitney engines and took off for a 60-second flight that covered about a mile. That was the only time the *Spruce Goose* ever flew. Its detractors claim that the controls shook so violently in Hughes' hands that he knew the plane would never be any good.

Hughes continued to pour money into the *Spruce Goose* for another 17 years, but the work steadily declined, and his orders that it be "ready to fly in 30 days" finally ended. Hughes never again made a major flight and his flying boat, like some mechanical alter ego, sat in closely guarded, climate-controlled seclusion for the rest of his life.

THE LOST ENDING OF *KUBLA KHAN*

A visit from a door-to-door salesman is generally unwelcome, but rarely as unwelcome as on one occasion in 1797.

Samuel Taylor Coleridge was recovering from an illness at an isolated farmhouse. He had taken two grains of opium ("for medicinal purposes"), which lulled him to sleep. He had a fantastic dream in which he composed a 300-line poem. When he awoke he hastened to pour onto paper the lines that were crystal clear in his mind. They began:

In Xanadu did Kubla Khan
A stately pleasure dome decree;
Where Alph, the sacred river, ran
Through caverns measureless to man,
Down to a sunless sea.

Coleridge had gotten 54 lines onto paper when he heard a knock on the door. Answering it, he was confronted by a traveling insurance salesman. As desperate as Coleridge was to get rid of the man, he was unable to do so for nearly an hour.

After the salesman left, Coleridge tried to recall the rest of his vision of the magical world of Xanadu, of which he had recorded only a fragment. He was unable to do so. He waited 20 years before publishing the part he had remembered, and it became one of his best-known works.

ROCKY ROAD TO RESPECT FOR THE *LAST SUPPER*

Leonardo da Vinci's *Last Supper* depicts Jesus and his apostles celebrating a Passover seder, sitting around a table as if on chairs. This is historically inaccurate: Jews at the Passover meal traditionally reclined on their sides around a low table. The

Last Supper as recreated by Hollywood.

painting also shows oranges being served. Oranges were not introduced into the Holy Land until long after Christ's death. (It could have been worse. A French artist later painted a version of the Last Supper in which cigarette lighters were included in the table setting.)

Though the *Last Supper* is now considered one of the world's greatest art treasures, the painting we see today is a heavily restored version of the original, which was unappreciated for most of its existence. A century after Leonardo painted it on the refectory wall of an Italian monastery, monks opened a doorway in the wall directly beneath Jesus, removing part of the table. The painting was never protected from dampness, which caused it to deteriorate badly. In 1796 Napoleonic troops quartered in the monastery used Christ's head for target practice.

FAMOUS LAST WORDS
A Brief Collection of Observations Better Left Unsaid

1864

"Come, come! Why, they couldn't hit an elephant at this dist..." were the last words of Union Major General John Sedgwick as he looked over a parapet at the Confederate lines during the Battle of Spotsylvania.

© WALT DISNEY PRODUCTIONS

1876

"I could whip all the Indians on the continent with the Seventh Cavalry," said George Armstrong Custer, turning down General Alfred Terry's offer of extra men and Gatling guns.

1912

"I cannot imagine any condition which would cause the ship to founder. I cannot conceive of any vital disaster happening to this vessel. Modern shipbuilding has gone beyond that," said Edward J. Smith, captain of the *Titanic.*

1927

"Goodbye, my friends, I'm off to glory," Isadora Duncan called out as she went for a ride in an open-topped Bugatti sports car. Seconds later the free-spirited dancer and choreographer was dead. Her long silk scarf had wrapped around the car's rear wheel and broken her neck.

1953

"I've had eighteen straight whiskeys—I think that's the record," were the last words of Welsh poet Dylan Thomas, celebrating his 39th birthday and the success of his *Collected Poems.* Thomas had always predicted he would die of "a massive alcoholic insult to the brain."

1955

"Take it easy driving. The life you save may be mine," was the message of a public service announcement James Dean record-ed two weeks before he was killed while speeding in his Porsche.

1971

While taping an episode of "The Dick Cavett Show," nutritionist and publisher of *Organic Gardening and Farming and Prevention* J. I. Rodale said, "I'm so healthy I expect to live on and on." Moments later he dropped dead of a heart attack.

LEANING TOWER STILL STANDS

The Leaning Tower of Pisa is probably the world's best-known,

longest standing monument to error. It was designed to be the bell tower for the cathedral at Pisa, and construction was begun in 1174. While it was still under construction, the builders realized they had a problem. A combination of soft soil and too shallow a foundation caused the tower to begin leaning to the south. Work was halted for a century. No one knew how to straighten the tower, but it was assumed that the tower had finally settled into place, so work proceeded, with the masons cutting their stones to accommodate the lean. When the tower was completed in 1350 it was a beautiful structure, eight stories tall, with graceful arches and marble columns. But it was its unique tilt that had already made it a tourist attraction, and it now attracts 1,500 visitors a day.

The leaning continues, at an average of one additional millimeter a year. There have been at least 17 attempts to hold the

tower in place. In 1934 concrete was forced into the ground beneath it, which only accelerated the drift. At present the top of the 179-foot tower is about 16 feet out of plumb. It is believed that another 6.6 feet remain before the Leaning Tower must finally fall. Optimists suggest that that could take another 2,000 years, while pessimists give it only another 30 or 40.

Pisa does not have Italy's only leaning tower. There are two twelfth-century towers in Bologna that stand not 20 feet apart and lean in opposite directions for a truly surreal effect. St. Mark's cathedral in Venice had a 325-foot bell tower with a lean of about 4 feet, which collapsed in 1902 after standing for over a thousand years.

LENIN—GOING, GOING, GONE?

Since his death in 1924, Lenin's pickled corpse has been on exhibit in a glass case in his tomb on Red Square. It is one of Moscow's most popular tourist attractions, and during the heyday of communism it was customary for newlyweds to visit Lenin's tomb immediately following their state-officiated marriage ceremonies to pay their respects. Lenin was the closest thing Russia had to a deity. So it was startling when in 1991 Peter Jennings announced, on the ABC Evening News, that the newly capitalist Soviet leaders had decided to auction off Lenin's body in order to raise funds. The minimum bid was to be $15 million. After the story appeared on ABC it was picked up by other news outlets, including *USA Today* and the Russian news agency *Tass*.

The Soviet Internal Affairs Minister denounced the story as a "brazen lie" and a "serious provocation." Meanwhile, the Russian Security Ministry began receiving offers from $1,000 to $27 million for Lenin's remains.

The story originally appeared in *Forbes* magazine's quarterly supplement, *FYI*, as a spoof on the Soviet move toward a market economy. Editor Christopher Buckley said he wanted to "test the limits of credulity" about events in the turbulent nation.

A few days later Jennings had to admit on the air that he had been gullible.

LICENSE PLATE: NONE

"NONE" was the word Skip Swenson of Los Angeles wanted to have on his vanity license plate in 1977. Shortly after he got it, he received a bill for $953 in unpaid parking tickets from Nevada. Swenson, who worked in Reno, Nevada, didn't realize that when filling out parking tickets the police write the word none in the space for the license plate number if the vehicle has none. Once Swenson got his custom plate the computers at last had a name to attach to all those outstanding tickets.

LAME LINES ABOUT LOST LIMBS

On the October 29, 1995, broadcast of NBC's "Meet the Press," host Tim Russert asked Senator Bob Kerrey (D-Nebraska): "Aren't you concerned that if you cut a deal with the Republicans, President Clinton will saw your limb off?"

Kerrey, a Medal of Honor winner whose leg had to be amputated after he stepped on a mine in Vietnam, seemed to enjoy Russert's mortification as he responded, "That's a terrible metaphor, since somebody's already sawed one of them off."

Admiral Horatio Nelson was the toast of England after his fleet trounced Napoleon's at the Battle of the Nile. As he made his way back to London for his hero's welcome, he rested at Yarmouth Inn for a night. The landlady was so ecstatic she asked his permission to rename her establishment The Nelson Arms.

"That would be absurd, seeing as I have but one," answered Nelson, who had lost his right arm in battle.

THE BLAZING BLADES OF DR. ROBERT LISTON

Before the introduction of anesthesia late in the nineteenth century, speed was the most highly regarded trait in a surgeon—if you know you're going to suffer, you at least want to suffer as briefly as possible. In the 1840s no surgeon was faster than Dr. Robert Liston, the First Professor of Clinical Surgery at University College Hospital in London. There was always a waiting list for his flashing blade, and he became a wealthy man. "Time me, gentlemen, time me!" he called out to students watching from the operating theater gallery as he pounced upon his fully conscious, strapped-down patients. Working with blade and saw, Liston could take off a leg in 2 $\frac{1}{2}$ minutes, and once removed a 45-pound scrotal tumor, whose owner had had to carry it around in a wheelbarrow, in four minutes flat. To free his hands, he would sometimes grip his bloody knife in his teeth.

Of course, speed had its price. During one of his 2 $\frac{1}{2}$-minute leg amputations, Liston inadvertently sliced off the patient's testicles as well.

In his most famous case Liston beat his advertised time, but the patient died of gangrene shortly afterward. In addition, he had cut off the fingers of his surgical assistant, who also later died of infection. While he was at it, his whipping blade had also slashed through the coattails of a colleague observing the operation. Convinced his vitals had been pierced, the man dropped dead on the spot from fright.

One operation—three fatalities. The record still stands.

LOOSE LIPS LOSE HEADS

During the terror following the French Revolution many of the nobility tried to escape the country, often in disguise. The Marquis de Condonset donned the ragged clothing of a peasant in order to avoid detection as he made his way to the border. He failed to fool anyone when he stopped at an inn full of real peasants, most of whom hadn't had a real meal in weeks, and imperiously ordered "an omelette made with a dozen eggs."

Old habits die hard, but the guillotine generally did the trick.

SPOTLIGHT ON LOUISIANA

Sheriff's deputies, game wardens and wildlife experts spent eight hours trying to rescue what they believed to be a black bear stuck 50 to 60 feet up in a pine tree near Shreveport,

Louisiana. After numerous tranquilizer darts failed to affect it, they discovered that the bear was actually a tattered black garbage bag that had gotten caught in the branches.

In November 1980 Texaco engineers set up a rig in the middle of Louisiana's Lake Peigneur and began drilling. The results were entirely unexpected. A whirlpool formed around the oil rig, into which began draining the entire contents of the 1,300-acre lake. Not only the water, but five houses, nine barges, eight tugboats, two oil rigs, a mobile home, and 10% of nearby Jefferson Island disappeared, leaving a crater a half-mile wide.

The Texaco engineers were unaware that there was an abandoned salt mine beneath their drilling rig.

A local fisherman said he had thought the world was coming to an end.

Lifeguards at the public pools in New Orleans were jubilant in 1985 when, for the first time, they got through the summer swimming season without a single drowning. A pool party was held to celebrate the accomplishment, with more than a hundred lifeguards and an equal number of guests in attendance.

Not in tune with the spirit of the festivities was one Jerome Moody, 31, whose body was found at the bottom of the pool after the party.

A Baton Rouge, Louisiana, man was sentenced to five years probation on a counterfeiting conviction. The punishment was mitigated by the unconvincing quality of the $20 bill he had tried to pass. He had cut the corners off a real $20 bill and pasted them onto the corners of a $1 bill. Federal Judge John Parker described him as "the most inept counterfeiter I ever heard of."

In 1989 attendants at a service station in Eunice, Louisiana, turned over the contents of the cash register, more than $100, to a naked man who claimed to have a gun in his pocket.

A LUXURY TAX WE COULDN'T AFFORD

The power to tax is the power to destroy, and it is a power that government sometimes wields thoughtlessly.

During the 1990 budget discussions, negotiators were unable to agree on higher taxes for the wealthy. Instead, in the name of tax fairness, they enacted a luxury tax that applied a 10% surtax on the indulgences of the rich: furs and jewelry over $10,000, automobiles over $30,000, yachts over $100,000 and private planes over $250,000. They estimated that the tax would bring in $1.5 billion over its five-year life span, on the assumption that the tax would not affect the way the rich spent their money. That assumption did not prove correct.

The yacht-building industry was particularly hard hit. Sales of high-priced boats fell by 80%. They say "a boat is a hole in the water into which you pour money," and it should be remembered that that money is being poured into the hands of other people. Expensive custom yachts turn out to be a fairly efficient means of redistributing wealth. A $1 million yacht requires 12,000 labor hours to build, or 8 worker years. Not only did some 25,000 skilled workers lose their jobs, but also the salesmen who sold the yachts and the marina workers who maintained them. Similar repercussions were felt in the private aircraft industry. It quickly became obvious that, far from raising revenue, the luxury tax was costing the government millions in unemployment compensation and lost income taxes.

Though everyone knew it had been a mistake, repealing the luxury tax was not easy. Because of the perverse way the government does its accounting, the luxury tax was still a money-maker on paper, based on the pretense that yacht sales had remained at their former levels. To take it off the books would require that a tax be raised elsewhere to make up for "lost" revenue. Clinton's 1992 tax increase provided the necessary cover, and the luxury tax was finally repealed in 1993.

The luxury tax provides a textbook example of the Law of Unexpected Consequences. Among the countless errors that government imposes on us, it is unique only in that it was quickly recognized and corrected.

COKE CANS THE MAGICAN

Some executive at Coca-Cola had a great idea for a promotional gimmick. Why not fill random cans with money and prize certificates? Customers would pop open their Cokes with a newfound excitement, hoping to be surprised by a $100 bill popping out on a special mechanism.

In 1990 Coca-Cola launched its $100 million MagiCan promotion, and shortly thereafter had to can it. The mechanism that was supposed to thrust the prizes out of the can when you opened it often failed, causing customers to get a surprise gulp of the foul-tasting chlorinated water that filled the can to give it weight.

MAGINOT LINE PROVES MARGINAL

To ensure that they would never again suffer the carnage of a German invasion, the French after World War I spent 12 years building a line of defensive fortresses along its border with Germany. Billions of francs were poured into the 87-mile system, the greatest defensive structure since the Great Wall of China. It was named the Maginot Line after André Maginot, the war minister.

The reinforced concrete forts bristled with everything from heavy artillery to machine guns. Hydraulic gun turrets rose to fire their howitzers, then lowered flush with their concrete casements in the event of bombardment. The fortresses were like self-contained cities; a Jules Verne world hundreds of feet below the surface provided living areas, hospitals and cinemas for 500,000 troops. Electric underground railways moved men and matériel, telephones linked the fortresses. The air-conditioning system was equipped with filters to guard against gas attacks.

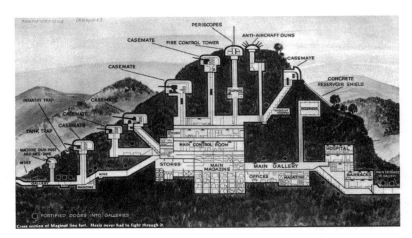

Cross section of Maginot line fort. Nazis never had to fight through it.

The seemingly impregnable Maginot Line caused France to think defensively rather than offensively, to concentrate on its shield rather than its sword. Napoleon would have reminded them that "the side that stays within its fortifications is beaten." Or, as General Patton put it, "Fixed fortifications are monuments to the stupidity of man."

When the Germans attacked France in 1940, they did so through France's unprotected border with Belgium. Ironically, though the fabled defensive line did the French no good, it was helpful to the Germans as they retreated in 1944; they used it against the American Third Army.

During the 1980s sections of the Maginot Line were auctioned off to German real estate developers for conversion into condominium units.

DISPOSSESSED OF HIS MANHOOD

Among early Christians, there were some radical sects that practiced self-castration as a way of controlling the desires of the flesh. This practice was ruled heretical by the Council of Nicea in A.D. 325, and Pope Leo I banned any priests from saying mass unless they were in possession of their manhood. In obedience to the letter, if not the spirit, of the law, one priest carried the withered remains of his former manhood in a snuff box. He was thus "in possession" of his manhood, at least until the snuff box was discovered by a small boy. Mistaking the contents for figs, the boy ate them.

MAJOR DIFFERENCES NOTED BETWEEN MAO VS. HITLER

In the 1960s editors of the Chinese Communist quarterly *National Construction* wanted to make it clear that China under Chairman Mao could in no way be confused with Germany under Adolf Hitler. They pointed out the striking dissimilarities between the two men:

"Adolf Hitler was 5 feet, 6 inches tall and weighed 143 pounds. He was renowned for his spellbinding oratory, relations with women, and annihilation of a minority people. In his last years, he suffered from insanity and delusions of grandeur. Chairman Mao is taller and heavier."

MARATHON MUDDLE IN MISSOURI: THE ST. LOUIS OLYMPICS, 1904

The marathon held at the Olympic Games hosted by St. Louis in 1904 is not likely to be mentioned among the great moments in international amateur competition.

The course was run on a humid, 90-degree afternoon over dusty, unpaved roads that featured seven hills. Of the 32 runners that set out, only 14 made it to the finish line. The rest had given up, choking on the dust raised by the procession of vehicles that accompanied them en route.

The first runner to return to the stadium, after a lengthy three hours, was Fred Lorz. Looking remarkably fresh, he gratefully acknowledged the crowd's ovation, posed for photos with President Roosevelt's daughter Alice and waited for his gold medal. His moment of glory ended when someone pointed out that he had ridden half the race in a car, and the real winner was still somewhere along the road, eating dust. Lorz admitted that he had gotten into a car after 9 miles, when he had suffered cramps. However, after he rode 11 miles the car broke down, at which point, fully recovered, he decided to run the rest of the way. He claimed he never meant to fool anyone, but couldn't resist basking a few minutes in the adulation of the crowd.

The real winner, Tom Hicks, staggered in shortly thereafter, enjoying a somewhat muted reception from the crowd that had given Lorz its all. Barely able to cross the finish line, he had to be carried to his dressing room, where it took four doctors to revive him in time to receive his gold medal. It turned out that Hicks had been fortified with brandy as well as egg whites laced with strychnine by his handlers during the race.

The entrant who probably should have won the marathon was the Cuban, Felix Carvajal. Carvajal, an amateur athlete in the best and worst sense of the term, had to hitchhike to the Games from New Orleans, cadging meals, after he lost all his money in a crap game. He was about to set out on the race in a long sleeved shirt, long pants and heavy boots until his rivals, feeling sorry for him, found him some lightweight shoes and suggested he cut off his shirt sleeves and the legs of his trousers. The 5-foot-tall Carvajal, a mailman in Cuba, easily kept the pace as more serious, better trained competitors dropped away. Unfortunately, his stomach finally got the better of him. He ate some peaches offered by a race official, then detoured into an orchard to snack on some apples. He soon developed stomach cramps and had to temporarily drop out of the race. Even so, he came in fourth. If he had laid off the snacks he would easily have won.

Another strong contender, a Zulu tribesman named Lentauw, came in a disappointing ninth. Most observers felt he would have done significantly better had he not lost nearly a mile when he was chased off course by a large, aggressive dog.

POLICE NOT ALWAYS ON TARGET

Most people assume that since police officers must carry sidearms on the job, they are skilled in their use, but skill with a firearm requires motivation and practice and many police officers are not so inclined. In 1993 the New York City Police Department proudly claimed it had improved its hit probability on violent felons to one hit per five shots. (It didn't mention where the other four shots ended up.)

A few years ago the *Washington Times* published a story that the District of Columbia police force had shot 126 people the previous year, making D.C. residents six times more likely to be shot by the police than New Yorkers. The police department quickly set the *Washington Times* straight. The police had fired their weapons on duty 126 times, but by no means were that many people shot. To begin with, 55% were accidental discharges. When the police intentionally shot at someone, they missed about 80% to 90% of the time. So of those 126 shots, less than 10 actually hit anyone. And that includes the two officers who shot themselves.

CHALLENGES TO A HAPPY MARRIAGE

Marriage is a struggle, but rarely more so than when you find out you inadvertently married someone of the same sex.

An unidentified 17-year-old woman in Memphis, Tennessee, sought an annulment of her four-month marriage in 1979 on the grounds that her husband was actually a 19-year-old woman. The bride claimed that her husband refused to undress in front of her, saying that he had a deformity as a result of a football injury. She also became suspicious when she overheard his parents calling him "Harriet."

In 1991 Bruce Jensen, 39, married Leasa Urioste, 34, in Lyman, Wyoming. Urioste claimed to be pregnant with twins, and Jensen evidently thought that he might be the father. Urioste later told Jensen the twins had been stillborn. After 3 $\frac{1}{2}$ years of marriage, Jensen sought an annulment on the grounds that he had discovered that Urioste was a man whose first name was actually Felix. The annulment was granted and Felix Urioste was sentenced to one year in prison for running up $40,000 to $50,000 in bills on Jensen's credit cards.

The marriage was "essentially celibate." Jensen was described by those who know him as "naive and sincere."

It *can* work, though. In 1989 popular jazz musician Billy Tipton died of bleeding ulcers at age 74. Tipton had been married 9 years, was a scoutmaster and raised three adopted sons. The funeral director preparing his body discovered Tipton was actually a woman. His widow had never guessed his secret—he had always claimed to have suffered a "sexually incapacitating injury." When given the news, one of the sons responded, "He'll always be Dad to us."

JIM MARSHALL'S MOST MEMORABLE TOUCHDOWN

The excitement of a sports event is that it's totally unscripted— there is no way to know what will happen next. That truth was impressed upon fans attending a game between the Minnesota Vikings and the San Francisco 49ers on October 25, 1964. They were present at a special moment in professional football, witnessing the kind of a play you remember for a lifetime.

Jim Marshall, a starting lineman with the Vikings, scooped up a 49ers' fumble and ran 66 yards. The fans roared, and above that roar Marshall was not able to hear the screams of his teammates. He was running toward the wrong goal line. For some reason, the fact that the tacklers he was skillfully evading were fellow Vikings failed to deter him. He scored two points for the 49ers, and was given a grateful embrace by Bruce Bosley of that team.

Marshall downplayed his feat with becoming modesty: "I just picked the ball up and started running. I guess I just got turned around."

As a result of his feat, Marshall enjoyed some popularity as a speaker at banquets and conventions.

MATISSE TURNS THE ART WORLD UPSIDE DOWN

On October 18, 1961, an exhibition of the work of the French master Henri Matisse opened at New York's Museum of Modern Art. One of the paintings, a 56-by-44 inch simple cut-and-pasted gouache called *Le Bateau*, (The Boat), was hung upside down and remained so for 47 days before anyone noticed. In that time an estimated 116,000 people had viewed the painting, including the artist's son, New York art dealer Pierre Matisse.

Mrs. Genevieve Habert, a Wall Street stockbroker, called the museum's attention to the improperly hung masterpiece in early December. She had visited the show three times and felt "vaguely disquieted." She found the reproduction of the painting correctly oriented in the show catalog. A museum guard insisted that the printer must have been the one in error. She then contacted the director, who realized she was right and corrected the problem in early December. The museum admitted that it had displayed paintings upside down three times before.

CLOSE ENOUGH FOR GOVERNMENT WORK...

In the 1880s, when the western border of South Dakota was being drawn, two surveyors worked toward each other, one from the north and one from the south. Both were supposed to be following the same meridian, but the surveyor who was working his way south missed the one who was working his way north by about a mile. In order to meet, the boundaries had to be joined with a slight east-west jog, visible on any map where the South Dakota border intersects the border of Montana and Wyoming.

In 1969 work crews in Pennsylvania were proceeding toward each other on a federally funded bridge and highway project when it was discovered that they would miss each other by 13 feet. Private consultants were blamed.

A two-lane bridge was built for a three-lane section of the state turnpike in West Virginia. Highway Department spokesman John Gallagher held designers responsible for the error, which no one noticed until after the bridge was built. "It sounds a lot worse than it is," Gallagher assured reporters.

MEDICAL QUESTIONNAIRE FOR ENGLISH-SPEAKING PATIENTS

English-language patients in post-war Japan were asked to answer the following questions on a medical form:

Are you haunted by horribles?

Do you ever run after your nose?

Does your nose choke?

Does your head or face or shoulder ever limp?

Has any part of your body suddenly grown uncontrollable?

Do you have heart thrills?

Do you have hot fit?

Do you have shiver of fingers?

Do you feel as if there were two when there is only one?

Are more than half your teeth off?

Do you ever have a drilling pain in your stomach?

Do your sholders or scruff of the neck grow stiff?

Do you always have trouble with your body?

Have you been influenced by atom bomb?

Did your doctor tell you you have abnormal body?

Have you been put into a mental hospital?

Do you readily become orderless unless you are strained?

SODA MACHINES KILL!

American soldiers know that they may be called upon at any time to give their lives for their country. Death may not necessarily come from a bullet, a mortar round or an artillery shell; today's soldier faces death in forms never before imagined. A report on one grave new peril appeared in a 1988 issue of the *Journal of the American Medical Association*. Dr. Michael Cosio of the Walter Reed Army Medical Center studied 15 cases in which male service personnel unsuccessfully engaged in combat with recalcitrant soda machines. Either angry over lost change or hoping to cadge a free drink, the servicemen shook and rocked the 1,000-pound machines, which then fell on top of them. Three died and 12 had to be hospitalized. Cosio also cited 32 civilian engagements, which resulted in eight deaths and 24 injuries. Judging by the statistics, military training does not provide much of an edge in soda machine combat.

FIRST MAN ON MOON MUFFS LINE

On July 20, 1969 Neil Armstrong stepped off the lunar module *Eagle*, and became the first man to set foot on the moon. He had a line ready for the occasion, "That's one small step for a man, one giant leap for mankind," but is it what he actually said? The millions who watched the transmission heard "That's one small step for man, one giant leap for mankind." Without the "a" the statement no longer makes sense, since "man" and "mankind" mean the same thing in that context. Armstrong claims that the statement was obscured by a burst of static, and the corrected version has gone into the history books.

The idea of traveling a quarter of a million miles to take the first step on another world, with the eyes of all mankind upon you, for then and for all time, only to blow your line—it's just too painful to imagine.

In an interview he gave British television, Buzz Aldrin, the second man to walk on the moon, described his own moment in history: "I held on to the near edge of the landing gear and checked my balance and then hesitated a moment...I am the first man to wet his pants on the moon."

The plaque that Neil Armstrong left on the moon contained a grammatical error. It was dated July 1969 A.D. "A.D." should be placed before, not after, the year it designates—the plaque should have read "July, A.D. 1969."

MOOSE, COW AFFAIR DOOMED FROM START

In Shrewsbury, Vermont, a lovelorn moose spent three months wooing a dairy cow, apparently unaware that they were of distinctly different and wholly incompatible backgrounds. Though Jessica the cow allowed the 700-pound bull moose to stand beside her and rest his head upon her back, she sternly rebuffed his numerous attempts to mount her.

Crowds of up to 4,000 people gathered alongside the pasture

to watch the doomed romance. One picture-taking tourist described the moose as "stupid-looking," prompting Jessica's owner, Larry Carrara, to pointedly note that the tourist was the one who'd driven hours to see the moose, not the other way around.

A local justice of the peace sought to cash in on the interest by performing a wedding ceremony for the two, but Carrara would not allow it. "I don't want no sideshow," he said, "I'm not going to allow it."

"Monster," a Galapagos tortoise at the Hogle Zoo in Salt Lake City, Utah, outdid the Vermont moose in picking unresponsive objects for his affections. He has variously directed his amorous attentions to a rock, a feeding pan and a garbage can lid. The zoo decided to seek a female of the appropriate species to keep Monster company.

THE BUG-INFESTED MOSCOW EMBASSY

When the United States needed a new embassy in Moscow in the 1970s, it decided to hire Soviet construction workers to build it. Employing American workers would have been cost-prohibitive as they would have had to have been flown to the USSR, housed there and paid extra for their troubles. The Soviet workers came a lot cheaper. It was assumed they would be up to their usual tricks, planting as many bugs as they could get away with, but American counterintelligence wasn't overly concerned. "Our assumption was that we could rectify what-ever the Soviets had done once we took control of the build-ing," said a senior State Department official. "That may have been too optimistic."

Optimistic is the word. When U.S. security experts checked out the finished eight-story building in 1985, they were stunned by its complete saturation with bugs, microphones and other suspicious devices. Tiny microphones were hidden everywhere. Normally these could be located by their wires, but the Soviets had put the wires inside steel reinforcing bars and beams where they couldn't be detected, reached or removed—there was no way to guess how many had gone undiscovered. There were thousands of electronic diodes mixed into the concrete—a sweep with a "nonlinear junction detector," or bug detector, would get back thousands of signals, making it impossible to locate the bugs. Inside the walls were small, empty metal cones attached to reinforcing rods arranged in peculiar ways, as if to form antennas. Experts theorized they were "passive" listening devices that could transmit sound when accessed with a microwave beam from the closed-up Russian Orthodox church across the street, which embassy officials dubbed "Our Lady of Eternal Vigilance."

"The whole building is nothing but an eight-story microphone plugged into the Politburo," commented a congressman. After spending millions of dollars on the new facility, the U.S. Embassy was never able to occupy it. One security man said we'd have to "destructively search" the building to find all the bugs. That's the kind of search you conduct with a wrecking ball. Congress eventually appropriated $240 million for a new building; perhaps the old one could be used as a broadcasting station for Radio Free Europe.

MOVIEMAKING MISTAKES

Since filming a single scene in a movie may require a number of separate shots, sometimes with a day off in between, inconsistencies crop up with props and costumes.

- When Bogart backhands Peter Lorre in *The Maltese Falcon*, snapping his head to the left, Lorre is wearing a polka-dot tie. When Lorre turns back, his tie has stripes. Say what you will for today's action heroes—only Bogie was tough enough to smack the polka dots off a necktie.

- Early in *Easy Rider*, after Peter Fonda makes a drug deal, he stashes his cash in his motorcycle's gas tank, and you can see he's wearing an expensive Rolex. Later, when he sets off on his search for America, he tosses his watch away to signify his contempt for the bourgeois restraints of, like, time and stuff. However, the watch he cavalierly tosses aside, which the camera zooms in on, is now a cheap Timex.

- In *Jailhouse Rock* Elvis is shown in an early scene wearing #6239 on his prison uniform, but later it's #6240, causing flub-spotter Bill Givens to wonder: Was he promoted for good behavior?

- In dramas set in the past, modernity occasionally puts in a surprise appearance. Sometimes it is hard to avoid—cavemen sport vaccination marks, ancient Romans benefit from modern dental work. Sometimes it is accidental but understandable—the elastic band of a barbarian's Jockey underwear momentarily peeks out above his loincloth. Sometimes, though, it is stupid and obvious, as in the case of historical characters inexplicably equipped with wristwatches. Some of the soldiers in *Spartacus* (1960) wear watches. The king in Cecil B. De Mille's *The Crusades* (1935) actually flips back his cloak to check the time. Still, little has equaled the combination of illogic and anachronism achieved in a scene in *The Ten Commandments* (1956) in which a *blind* man is shown wearing a wristwatch.

MYSTERIOUS STONE TABLET YIELDS MESSAGE FROM THE PAST

Archaeologists dug up a mysterious carved stone tablet among the prehistoric relics in the Grave Creek Mound in West Virginia in 1838. The carving on the tablet was completely inscrutable to scientists who studied it over the next century. Altogether, over 60 linguists examined it, trying to decipher the hieroglyphics on its surface. There was speculation that the tablet might be Runic or Etruscan in origin, leading to further questions as to how it could possibly have been left among the Native American relics in the mound.

In 1930 a young man photographing the famous mystery relic found the solution. Like the common children's puzzle in which greatly elongated letters can be read only when they're viewed at a sharp angle, the lettering was quite legible in the young man's photograph, which was taken from an oblique perspective. The stone read:

BILL STUMP'S STONE
OCTOBER 14, 1838

LOST IN SPACE WITH NASA

The *Mariner* probe was supposed to reach Venus after a 100-day space flight, then go into orbit, sending back scientific data. The spacecraft was launched from Cape Canaveral on July 22, 1962, but veered dangerously off course as it separated from its booster. Four minutes after the launch, NASA officials had to press the destruct button and blow up the $18.5 million spacecraft. A subsequent investigation showed that the navigational error was caused by the omission of a single minus sign on a computer program, one of the more expensive typos on record.

On April 24, 1990, the Hubble space telescope was put into orbit. The public was told that the $1.6 billion telescope would provide a clearer view of the universe than had ever been possible, but it soon developed that the Hubble had a serious case of myopia. A special space shuttle mission had to fit it with a corrective lens. Cost? About $86 million. If the error had been detected prior to its launch, it could have been corrected for about $2 million, but optical tests were not run in order to save money.

The original error had occurred in 1980 when technicians building the telescope filled a gap in an optical testing device they were using with three small washers. Cost? About 25¢ each.

The $980 million *Mars Observer* was launched in 1992 to orbit and photograph the red planet. In August 1993 it was 450 million miles into its mission, about to go into Mars' orbit, when NASA lost contact with it. An investigative panel speculated that the problem was a ruptured fuel line, as the spacecraft was programmed to pressurize its fuel tanks at that point. Originally the pressurization was supposed to take place five days into the mission, but NASA changed that to 11 months to avoid a possible leak. Since the valves were not designed with the later schedule in mind, it is believed that the change of plans caused the disaster.

NIXON, RICHARD; THE WIT AND WISDOM OF

After a motorcycle policeman in Nixon's official escort was injured, and he was lying in the road awaiting medical attention, Nixon asked him, "How do you like your job?"

When Nixon arrived at the Paris airport for the funeral of French President Pompidou, Nixon declared, "This is a great day for France!"

A man who made a chair out of a single piece of wood wished to present it to President Nixon, and was invited to the Oval Office to do so. When Nixon tried the chair, it immediately collapsed beneath him. Nixon got up from the floor, brushed himself off and asked the man, "Well, how do you go about doing this kind of work?"

In the few minutes before beginning a TV interview with David Frost, Nixon turned to his host and offered this casual ice-breaker: "Well, did you do any fornicating this weekend?"

THE LONG, LONELY WAR OF HIROO ONODA

As they say in the army, "there's always someone who doesn't get the word..."

For Hiroo Onoda, World War II did not end until March 9, 1974. That was the day he left the jungle on the island of Lubang in the Philippines, concluding a war he had waged since 1944. He wrote an account of his experience, aptly titled *No Surrender.*

Onoda was stationed on Lubang with orders to organize Japanese troops for guerrilla warfare after the American invasion. When the Americans came, it was with a force that quickly overwhelmed Japanese resistance and astonished Onoda. He could hardly believe it when he saw naval guns brought to bear on a single Japanese soldier exposed on the beach. A rifle, a machine gun, even a mortar against a single soldier he could comprehend—but a five-inch cannon? As the U.S. Marines moved onto the island, he was again stupefied. He would come across scenes of engagements where the bodies of Japanese littered the terrain along with discarded chewing gum wrappers. "Here we were holding on for dear life, and these characters were chewing gum while they fought!" he observed pathetically.

Onoda gathered a team of four Japanese survivors and headed for the hills. They survived on caches of rice, as well as bananas, coconut milk and an occasional cow rustled from the islanders. When the rice ran out they "liberated" what they could.

Years went by, and the team continued to patrol Lubang, harassing the islanders and gathering intelligence for the Japanese counterattack they convinced themselves was inevitable. Onoda had been warned by his superior officer that his mission might take years but had been assured, "Whatever happens, we'll come back for you." When leaflets were dropped telling the four men the war was over, they chalked it all up to clever U.S. propaganda.

One member of the team, regarded as something of a weak reed by the others, surrendered in 1949. Another was shot and killed in a skirmish in 1954. After that engagement Japan launched an enormous effort to get Hiroo and his surviving associate, Kozuka, out of the jungle. Onoda's family visited the island; left personal letters, photos and mementos; and broadcast appeals over loudspeakers—all to no avail. By this time the two holdouts were impervious to evidence—everything was regarded as a clever forgery. A small grammatical error in a personal letter or an unrecognized element in a family photo was taken as proof of a trick. When they found stacks of Japanese newspapers left for them, they assumed that they were specially printed up by the Americans, including a good deal of authentic information but carefully excising accounts of the war's progress. The fact that there were photos of Tokyo teeming with life was enough to give the lie to any claim that the war was over—for hadn't the Japanese sworn to fight to the last man, woman and child? When Onoda's brother stood in a clearing for weeks, calling to him over a loudspeaker, Onoda watched from the cover of the jungle and marveled at the cleverness of the impersonation. When he heard his brother's voice finally crack with emotion, Onoda snorted to himself, "The impostor couldn't keep it up." Clearly Onoda had a willful desire to believe his fantasy, a desire fed by the enormous psychic price he would have to pay for giving it up.

In 1972 his friend Kozuka was killed in another firefight. Once again, the manhunt for Onoda intensified, but he evaded it easily. Two years later he came across a young Japanese globetrotter, Norio Suzuki, who had camped in the woods hoping to find the mysterious warrior. Onoda claimed to have been reassured that Suzuki was no spy by the fact that he was wearing sandals with heavy woolen socks. No one but an authentic Japanese would do something so incongruous, he reasoned. Perhaps lonely after two years of solitary duty, Onoda struck up a conversation and was won over by the ingenuous Suzuki. Still, though, he would not leave—only a direct order from his commanding officer would persuade him to do so. On March 9, his former commanding officer, Major Yoshimi Taniguchi, now a bookseller, came to Lubang.

Meeting him in a jungle clearing, Onoda snapped to attention and barked out, "Lieutenant Onoda, sir, reporting for orders."

Major Taniguchi formally ordered him to cease all combat activity.

There is a hallowed place in Japanese tradition for those who pursue futile quests in the name of honor, and when Onoda returned home he was celebrated as a hero. He was grateful but somewhat bewildered. As he wrote, "For thirty years I had thought I was doing something for my country, but now it looked as though I had just caused a lot of people a lot of trouble."

DON'T YOU HATE IT WHEN THAT HAPPENS!?

The Anti-Careless Accident Campaign of Southwestern Australia sponsored a publicity stunt in which a hospital bed was pushed the 2,000 miles from Hobart to Perth. During the journey, one of the nurses pushing the bed fell under the casters and broke her neck.

In 1990 ABC's "20/20" ran an interview with the actor who played Buckwheat in the "Our Gang" comedies. Afterward it was discovered that the actor who had actually portrayed Buckwheat had died 10 years earlier.

For years an exclusive men's club in Washington, D.C., had been selling a custom-designed club tie to its members. In 1994 the tie was hastily withdrawn after a British visitor informed the club that its emblem incorporated the bar sinister, a heraldic device used to indicate bastardy.

Mexico's most wanted criminal, a man believed to be responsible for 20 murders, was finally captured after he had eluded the authorities for many years. He had joined the police force under an assumed name, and shortly before his arrest had been promoted to captain.

Half of the original manuscript for *Of Mice and Men* was destroyed before Steinbeck had completed it. The legendary excuse was valid in this case—his dog had eaten it.

The house of Chanel was forced to destroy hundreds of garments and offer apologies to Muslims in 1994 after it discovered it had unwittingly decorated a line of bustiers with verses from the Koran.

Wine merchant William Sokolin had paid $300,000 for a 1787 bottle of Chateaux Margaux once owned by Thomas Jefferson. He presented it before a group of 300 wine collectors at Manhattan's Four Seasons restaurant in 1989, hoping that one of them might offer $519,000 for it. Before bidders could get out their checkbooks, he dropped the bottle and broke it.

LITTLE-KNOWN HAZARDS OF ORAL HYGIENE

While conscientiously practicing oral hygiene, Kerry Shea, 14, of DePere, Wisconsin, swallowed her toothbrush. She explained that she was "brushing the back of my tongue because I saw on TV that it helps to get a lot of sugar that way," when "it just slipped and I swallowed it." A doctor was able to retrieve it.

According to an article in the March 1988 *Archives of Surgery*, there were only 31 cases on record of toothbrushes being swallowed in the United States. Strangely, of those 31 instances, four occurred in 1986 in the town of Durham, North Carolina.

THE OUTHOUSE CLOSES ITS DOORS

The obvious association between two major bodily functions must have inspired Gordon and Jasmine Geisbrecht to open a restaurant outside of Winnipeg, Manitoba, with the theme of toilets. Opened in 1986, The Outhouse featured toilet bowls scattered around the dining room as decor, and the menus displayed a toilet seat logo.

Health inspectors forced the restaurant to close because it lacked adequate bathrooms.

LOSS OF PANTS

In the Miami Miller Lite Bowling Tournament of 1984, pro

bowler Mark Baker made an embarrassing split—down the seat of his pants. Baker was going for a strike in the 10th frame, so he "put something extra" in his throw. That something extra tore open the seat of his pants in front of the standing-room-only crowd. He got his strike and was feeling elated, when he heard a woman say, "My, what a white ass he has."

As Baker put it, "Being from California, I wasn't a big believer in underwear."

On the tournament circuit, Baker picked up the nickname "Moon." He received 17 pairs of underwear by mail from concerned women around the country.

Not many track-and-field stars are capable of jumping right out of their pants, but Lane Lohr managed the feat at the 1985 NCAA meet in Austin, Texas. Lohr, a University of Illinois pole vaulter, had just cleared the bar at 17 feet, 2 inches, when a gust of wind blew his pole underneath him. It slid up the side of his shorts and tore them off as he fell into the pit. After a moment of stunned silence, the stadium erupted in cheers as he grabbed a towel to wrap around himself.

A woman sued the Rite Aid Pharmacy in Shelton, Connecticut for $15,000, claiming that a floor polisher there tore her pants off. In her claim, Bette Northrup said that she was reaching for

a pair of pantyhose behind the polisher when she tripped over its cord. In order to keep from falling, she grabbed it and accidentally turned it on. It then "lurched, vibrated, spun around and moved violently out of control with great force," according to her suit, tearing her pants and stockings off.

What could be less funny than a Communist Party show trial? Strangely enough, a party purge in Czechoslovakia in November 1952 had one light moment.

The former government officials had spent two years in prison undergoing reeducation. On the day of their trial, they were given back their old civilian clothing and taken to court. The former Moravian party secretary, Ota Sling, had been quite overweight before his arrest, but had slimmed down in prison. As he stood before the court, he raised his arms to make a gesture, causing his oversized trousers to drop to his ankles. Judges, guards, defense counselors and defendants all burst out laughing, though Sling's prosecutor took the incident as a personal affront.

BRING ME YOUR POOR, YOUR TIRED, YOUR ANIMAL PESTS...

Some of the pests that plague the United States were deliberately introduced here.

- California loses millions of dollars in produce due to the numerous descendants of snails brought here by a French immigrant in the 1850s, Antoine Delmas. He was fond of *escargot*, and wanted to assure himself a supply in his new home.

- Gypsy moth caterpillars periodically defoliate millions of acres of forests in New England, causing large numbers of trees to die. The caterpillar was imported into the United States from France by a Medford, Massachusetts, naturalist in 1869. He had hoped to cross it with the American silk moth in order to produce a hardy thread-making variety.

- The nutria, a 15-pound rodent related to the rat, has ravaged the vegetation in coastal marshes in the American South, causing erosion and flooding problems. The animal was introduced into the United States to support the fur trade. Now

Louisiana is sponsoring cooking contests with the nutria as the main course, hoping people might reduce the pest's population by eating them.

- The grackle, a winged pest that emits a grating screech and does considerable damage to crops, was brought to the United States from England for the most poetic of motives. In the 1890s philanthropist Eugene Schifflin decided that a fitting tribute to Shakespeare would be to introduce into the United States every bird specifically mentioned in one of the Bard of Avon's plays. Not every bird he brought over adapted, but the grackles multiplied *ad infinitum*, to the extent that the government has to launch occasional extermination drives.

- Killer bees are all descendants of 26 queen bees from Africa, brought to the Western Hemisphere in the 1950s by a Brazilian geneticist, Warwick Kerr. He planned to study whether crossbreeding Brazilian bees with the African variety would create better honey producers. Bees that escaped from Kerr's São Paulo laboratory spread over Brazil and are now moving into the United States.

PETROGLYPHS EXCITE PARK RANGERS

Excitement swept the Forest Service in 1987 when a series of petroglyphs were discovered in the Siskiyou National Forest in Oregon. According to archaeologists, the carvings, on three separate boulders, looked like the work of early tribes that had inhabited the region. Work began on a visitors' center that would protect the carvings as well as display them and explain their significance to interested scholars, tourists and student groups.

Work on the center was suspended when artist Jeff Kerker came forward and explained that he had carved the petroglyphs a few years earlier. He had been curious to see how long it would take to make them, and found he was able to finish them in one afternoon.

"I wasn't trying to fool anyone," he explained.

OOPS! SPECIAL SECTION: PRIZE-WINNING PHONIES

"GIRL YOU KNOW IT'S TRUE"—OR IS IT?

In 1989 the Grammy Award for "Best New Artist" went to two people who couldn't sing. It's not that Rob Pilatus and Fab Morvan couldn't sing in the sense that an audiophile might say Madonna can't sing—they couldn't sing at all.

Earlier, Rob and Fab had approached German record producer Frank Farian, hoping to get a record contract. With their buffed-up bodies and androgynous good looks, Farian quickly decided that the unemployed models would go farther on appearance than talent. As Rob himself had once observed, "I looked at all the superstars. What is their different thing? Their hair...I wanted to be a star. I said, 'I have to fix my hair.'" Farian set them up with $750 hair extensions, called them Milli Vanilli, and had them lip-synch to "Girl You Know It's True," a song that had already been recorded by studio musicians. When the album become one of the biggest hits of 1988, selling 10 million copies, the two went on a concert tour, lip-synching all the way.

Fab and Rob seemed to become a bit enraptured with their own hype. "This is for all the artists out there. Never give up on your dreams," said one of them as he accepted the Grammy. Then they made a real mistake. The ruse could have continued for some time, but they began insisting that Farian use their voices in the follow-up album, a demand he refused. Finally Farian held a press conference on November 4, 1990, and spilled the beans. The Grammy was repossessed.

Fab and Rob promised to record an album "with our own voices on it, which will prove our talent." We're still waiting.

THE EDUCATION OF LITTLE TREE: HEARTWARMING TALE GIVES HEARTBURN

In the 1970s Forrest Carter enjoyed considerable success as an author. *The Rebel Outlaw: Josey Wales*, was later made into a Clint Eastwood film. *The Education of Little Tree*, the heartwarming memoir of his Native American upbringing, was a natural for the multicultural market that was beginning to develop. First published in 1976, it was universally acclaimed, spending 14 weeks at the top of the *New York Times* paperback bestseller list. It won the 1991 Abby Award. One critic wrote, "It addresses concerns of environment, family, racism and human relations which—when misunderstood or ignored—can cause catastrophic results."

As it turned out, Carter knew something about that. To the shock and dismay of those who had admired the book, Carter turned out to be a fraud, and a particularly brazen one. Though his dust-jacket bio described him as a Cherokee Indian who had worked as a cowboy before trying his hand at writing, a distant relative broke the news: His real name was Asa Earl Carter, described by author Bob Tamarkin as "a Ku Klux Klan terrorist, right-wing radio announcer, homegrown American fascist and anti-Semite, rabble-rousing demagogue" and speechwriter for Alabama's segregationist Governor Wallace in the early 1960s. In his 30 years as a member of the Ku Klux Klan, Carter was suspected of involvement in many violent acts, including an assault that left two other Klan members critically wounded. The pseudonym under which his gentle ode to Native American life was published was taken from the name of Nathan Bedford Forrest, Confederate Army general and founder of the KKK.

"JIMMY'S WORLD" DISCOVERED IN WASHINGTON, D.C.

In 1981 the Pulitzer Prize for journalism went to Janet Cooke of the *Washington Post* for a gripping feature she'd written entitled "Jimmy's World." Jimmy was an eight-year-old African-American in an urban nightmare of drugs and squalor. His mother was an ex-prostitute, his father a drug dealer and Jimmy himself a heroin addict since he was five. Jimmy's thin little arms were covered with needle marks; his own father shot him up, saying, as if he was helping him tie his shoes, "Pretty soon, you got to learn how to do this for yourself."

Cooke's poignant account sparked a public outcry, and the police felt pressured to find little Jimmy and deliver him from his world. All the while, though, they smelled something fishy. None of their contacts on the street had heard of Jimmy, or anyone like him. And what junkie would give heroin away free for three years? After a three-week investigation, the police concluded that "the child, as described, did not exist." Janet Cooke stood her ground and claimed she couldn't identify the people she'd written about, not only for First Amendment reasons, but because drug dealers had threatened her life. The *Washington Post* continued to defend her, and six months later she received her Pulitzer.

With all the publicity that "Jimmy's World" attracted, Janet's own world came under a harsh spotlight. It turned out she'd lied about her academic credentials on her resumé. Cooke finally confessed that she'd made up the entire story.

Strangely enough, not long afterward a student in Richard Astle's creative writing class at San Diego State University turned in an essay titled "Anthony's World," which, with the exception of a change of name, age and locale, was plagiarized word for word from Ms. Cooke's *Washington Post* article. Before Mr. Astle discovered the offense, he had given the story a B instead of an A because he felt it read more like a newspaper article than a piece of creative writing. Then, as Astle tells it, the student "came up after class and argued that he deserved a better grade. He said he needed the grade to get into law school."

PLANES, TRAINS AND AUTOMOBILES

In 1972 China bought 10 Boeing 707s, along with 40 Pratt & Whitney replacement engines, a much higher number than would be normally needed. In 1980 it was discovered that Chinese aeronautical engineers had secretly built an exact copy of the passenger jet, which they fitted with the replacement engines and called the Y-10. Since the engineers had failed to properly establish its center of balance, though, the Y-10 was unable to fly.

Concerned about employee pilferage of the miniature liquor bottles served to passengers, security officials at Pan Am equipped the liquor cabinets with a special device that would record the exact times when the cabinet was opened, to help to identify the thieves. Crews were not told about it, as that would defeat its purpose. Susan Becker, a stewardess, noticed one of the devices during a flight and suspected it was a bomb. She alerted the pilot, who made an emergency landing of the Boeing 707. The 80 passengers aboard were told to leave through emergency exits.

The cost of the emergency landing was nearly $20,000.

The miniature bottles of liquor sold for 50¢ each.

USAir sent a letter to a college student welcoming him to its frequent-flier program. Evidently, they were unaware that the student had died weeks earlier in a USAir plane that had crashed at New York's LaGuardia Airport.

After a yearlong investigation, the U.S. Air Force revealed the reason why an $18 million F-16 had crashed in September 1992. The pilot, Lieutenant Colonel Don Snelgrove, was evidently distracted while attempting to urinate in his plastic "piddle pack."

When railroad engineer Donald Silk felt a hankering for a candy bar while traveling through the town of Gardner, Massachusetts, he thought he could safely leave his train on the tracks for a few minutes to get it. After he left it, the idling train slipped into gear and began moving down the track without him. Silk hailed a police officer, Robert Babineau, and the two raced by squad car through three towns trying to intercept the unmanned six-car train at crossings.

After the train had traveled out of control for 30 miles, dispatchers shunted it onto a spur where it was allowed to slam into empty boxcars, forcing it to a stop.

On May 24, 1974, Biagio di Crescenzio was driving near Fondi, a small town about 60 miles from Rome, when he skidded off the road and hit a tree. A passing motorist took the badly injured di Crescenzio to the Fondi Hospital for treatment. Doctors at the Fondi Hospital decided that di Crescenzio was so seriously injured that he required special treatment available only in Rome.

They sent him off in an ambulance, which got only a few miles outside of Fondi when it collided with an oncoming car. A motorist who witnessed the wreck took di Crescenzio to the hospital in nearby Latina.

Doctors there, recognizing the seriousness of his condition, sent him in another ambulance to Rome. Ten miles from Latina the ambulance skidded into oncoming traffic. Biagio di Crescenzio was killed.

A Spanish air force jet shot itself down on August 7, 1979, when shells it was firing into a hillside target site ricocheted back. The pilot ejected safely.

After a Russian Aeroflot passenger jet crashed in Siberia on March 22, 1994, killing all 75 people aboard, the plane's black box tapes were recovered. They indicated that just prior to the crash the pilot, Yaroslav Kudrinsky, had been giving his two children a flying lesson. The last words on the tape were from the pilot's 12-year-old daughter, who asked, "Daddy, can I turn this?"

Three high school football players were struck and killed by cars while imitating a scene from a 1993 movie, *The Program*, in which a coach makes his players lie down on the center line of a busy highway in order to prove their nerve. Whether this could be blamed totally on the movie was open to question, however. In 1986 the *New York Times* reported that dozens of rural Americans were run over and killed annually after they got drunk and lay down in the middle of the highway.

POLITICAL CORRECTNESS RUN AMUCK

Some sort of political-correctness program must have been operating on automatic in the computers at the *Fresno Bee* in 1991. Referring to the budget crisis in Massachusetts, instead of writing that new taxes would soon put the state back in the black, the newspaper reported that they would put it "back in the African-American."

A British chess enthusiast and illustrator had a wonderful idea—a children's book that would bring chess pieces to life and involve them in an adventure. And so he produced *The Amazing Adventures of Dan the Pawn*, in which a white pawn named Dan is the hero of the chessboard as he defends his king against the Black Army.

Sadly, the artist failed to consider the book's political implications. The National Union of Teachers' official journal, *Teacher*, decried his book as racist. You see, the white pieces defeated the black ones.

At the Odd Ball Cabaret in North Hills, Los Angeles, customers paid $20 each to watch a nude dancer bathe in a glass-sided shower on its stage. A complaint was lodged by the Los Angeles Disabled Access Appeals Commission, which charged that the attraction must shut down unless it provided wheelchair access for the performers. The club had never employed a wheelchair-bound dancer and felt it was unlikely to do so in the future, but was unable to soft-soap the commission.

"It doesn't matter what you're doing. You can't discriminate against the physically disabled," said Ron Shigeta, chief of the Disabled Access Division of the city's Department of Building and Safety, clearly in a lather.

POSTAGE DUE

Hubert Humphrey had a stamp issued in his honor in 1991. 300 million of them were printed before a small error was noticed—the stamps had the wrong starting date for Humphrey's term as vice president. The stamps had to be destroyed, at a loss of $380,000.

Bill Picket, an African-American cowboy and rodeo star, was included in a special stamp series entitled "Legends of the West." Once the design was unveiled, though, Picket's descendants told the Postal Service that it had portrayed not Bill, but his brother Ben, and they wanted the error rectified. The stamps had already been printed and shipped to post offices but not yet officially put on sale. The Postal Service recalled the stamps, at a cost of $1.1 million. It then turned out that a few post offices had jumped the gun and sold some sheets of the stamps, some 183 in all. These sheets of stamps, sold for $5.80 apiece, are now among the rarest in existence, valued at up to $12,500. The Postal Service tried to recover the sets it had sold, making one purchaser an offer he must have found hard to refuse—a $5.80 refund, *plus* an official U.S. Postal Service coffee mug. He politely declined.

Between 1991 and 1995, the Postal Service produced commemorative sheets for the 50th anniversary of World War II. Most were bland, along the lines of "Bonds and stamps help war effort," but in 1994 a stamp displaying a lurid mushroom cloud over Hiroshima was canned after the Japanese government protested. Many customers might have found the A-bomb stamp a welcome counterpoint to the cutesy "love" stamps, and well suited to affixing to their Form 1040 tax return envelopes.

In Italy the postal service discovered that over 200 cards and letters had passed undetected through the system with such fake commemorative stamps as "Stolen Car Week," "200 Years of the *Camaro* [the Mafia]," and "Naples' Tainted and Muddy Water Supply." Others honored porn stars and gangsters. The stamps had been in use for more than a year. Three people were arrested.

THE GOLDEN BANANA PEEL

Second Place: Sam Goldwyn

One of Hollywood's most prominent producers for 30 years, Polish-born Sam Goldwyn never fully mastered the English language. Goldwyn became so legendary for his malapropisms that his stable of writers used to coin them for the fan magazines, just to needle him. Thus, not everything regarded as a Goldwynism can be authenticated. Nevertheless, these are among the classics for which he is famous:

"Anybody who goes to see a psychiatrist ought to have his head examined."

Referring to a script he had been given, Goldwyn is supposed to have said: "I read all of it part of the way through."

"I'll write you a blanket check."

"Why call him Joe? Every Tom, Dick and Harry is called Joe."

"I don't think anybody should write his autobiography until after he's dead."

"A verbal contract isn't worth the paper it's written on."

"It's more than magnificent; it's mediocre."

"Let's have some new clichés."

"I'll give you a definite maybe."

"He's living beyond his means, but he can afford it."

"I never put on a pair of shoes until I've worn them five years."

"I don't care if my pictures don't make a dime, so long as everyone comes to see them."

"I had a monumental idea this morning, but I didn't like it."

FUMBLING THE PRESIDENT'S FOOTBALL

To launch a nuclear strike requires "the football," actually a locked briefcase, which the Secret Service is supposed to keep near the president at all times. Inside the briefcase is a code-book listing a variety of nuclear strike options that he must issue to the Pentagon in order to authorize a strike. Even at the height of the Cold War, the football was not always within the president's reach. It was once left behind on Air Force One during Gerald Ford's trip to France. Jimmy Carter refused to let the military set up a trailer on his property at Plains, Georgia, where he often vacationed, and the agent with the football had to stay in Americus, 10 miles away. Ronald Reagan also became separated from the football when he was trapped for a period in a broken White House elevator. George Bush was once in such a hurry to play tennis after attending church that he left the aide with the football behind. The Secret Service had to dispatch a car to pick him up.

AN INSPIRING PROCESSION

Late in the sixteenth century, religious processions were held on holy days at the Hereford Cathedral in England. The Dean of Hereford, a Dr. Price, decided that he should no longer march with those of lesser importance but, in view of his higher status, should ride on horseback. On horseback he could also more easily inspire the crowd by reading from his prayer book, he felt.

On the glorious day, the cleric got on his high horse, opened his prayer book and set out with the procession. He hadn't gotten very far when a stallion, inspired less by the dean's religious devotion than by his mare, broke loose and mounted her. In this fashion the three of them proceeded down the street with the dean trapped and unable to get very much reading done.

PEERLESS PROGNOSTICATIONS

"Nothing of importance happened today."
—Diary entry for July 4, 1776, by King George III of England

"Radio has no future."
"Heavier-than-air flying machines are impossible."
"X-rays will prove to be a hoax."
—Lord Kelvin, President of the Royal Society (1890-1895)

"Nothing has come along that can beat the horse and buggy."
—Businessman Chauncey Depew, warning his nephew not to invest $5,000 with Henry Ford, then an unknown ex-bicycle repairman with big ideas

"There is as much chance of repealing the Eighteenth Amendment prohibition of alcohol as there is for a hummingbird to fly to the planet Mars with the Washington Monument tied to his tail."
—Senator Morris Sheppard, author of the 18th Amendment introducing Prohibition

"I have seen the future, and it works."
—Lincoln Steffens, American social reformer, after his visit to communist Russia in 1919

"No Civil War picture ever made a nickel."
—MGM production chief Irving Thalberg, turning down the rights to Margaret Mitchell's *Gone with the Wind*

"I believe it is peace for our time...peace with honor."
—Great Britain's Prime Minister Neville Chamberlain in 1938,

after signing the Munich Agreement ceding the Sudetenland to Hitler

"Atomic energy might be as good as our present day explosives, but it is unlikely to produce anything very much more dangerous."
—Winston Churchill, 1939

"Someday the American people will erect a monument to his memory."
—Eddie Rickenbacker, American World War I ace, on Senator Joe McCarthy

Jesse Jackson predicted that with his acquittal, O.J. Simpson could become a strong voice in the fight against domestic violence.

UNEXPLAINED FEATS OF THE PSYCHIC MASTERS

Danish astronomer Tycho Brahe (1546-1601), whose precise observations of the stars paved the way for the discoveries of Kepler and Newton, also dabbled in astrology. He used his studies of the heavens to predict the exact date on which the sultan of the Ottoman Empire, Süleyman the Magnificent, would die.

After he released his prediction he learned that Süleyman the Magnificent had died some time previously.

A Hindu yogi named Rao promised to put on a miraculous display in Bombay, India, in 1966. Six hundred members of Bombay's social elite were invited to witness the holy man actually walk on water. Tickets were sold for $100 each, and the event was covered by *Time* magazine. The bearded mystic in his flowing saffron robes prayed silently at the edge of the pond, preparing himself for the feat. When all the forces were properly aligned, he boldly stepped forward and immediately plunged beneath the surface.

Russian psychic E. Frenkel claimed to have stopped moving bicycles and cars with his mental powers. In a public demonstration of his psychic prowess, he stood astride railroad tracks in order to stop a moving train. He should have stuck with bicycles.

A British stage hypnotist who performed under the name Romark gave a public demonstration of his psychic prowess on October 12, 1977. Having announced that he would drive a car, blindfolded, through the town of Ilford, he performed an elaborate ritual to assure the crowd that there would be no possible cheating. He first placed a coin and then a wad of bread dough over each closed eye, and held them down with a wide cloth band wrapped around his head. He then climbed into a yellow Renault and headed down the town's main street, his steering guided only by his uncanny "second sight."

After 20 yards Romark slammed into the back of a parked police van. Romark later explained that "that van was parked in a place that logic told me it wouldn't be."

In 1987 a Ugandan priestess, Alice Lakwena, led an uprising called the Holy Spirit Movement. She claimed to have developed an ointment that, if spread over their bodies, would protect her followers from bullets. Those few of her followers who survived their next battle with government troops had excellent grounds for a class action suit.

PSYCHOLOGICAL WARFARE, IRAQI STYLE

During the Persian Gulf War, the Iraqis attempted to demoralize American GIs with their own version of World War II's "Axis Sally" radio broadcasts, dubbed "Baghdad Betty." The attempt suffered from a lack of crosscultural understanding though, as in this taunt: "GI, you should be home. Why? Because while you are away, movie stars are taking your women. Robert Redford is dating your girlfriend. Tom Selleck is kissing your lady. Bart Simpson is making love to your wife."

PURVIS' FOLLY

As head of the Chicago office of the FBI, Melvin Purvis was second in rank and renown only to J. Edgar Hoover. His investigative technique was characterized less by finesse than by copious applications of firepower. John Dillinger and Pretty Boy Floyd were among the notorious gangsters whose careers he ended in a hail of lead. It wasn't only in matters of law enforcement that Purvis displayed a certain lack of subtlety. He also achieved renown for producing the first belch broadcast on national radio. While making a guest appearance on a radio show sponsored by Fleischmann's yeast in 1935, he resonantly burped in the middle of delivering a commercial. For years afterward Fleischmann's carried the nickname "Purvis' Folly."

Melvin Purvis

RAINMAKER WASHES OUT

Rainmaker Charles M. Hatfield was hired by the city of San Diego to end its drought in 1915. The Morena and Otay reservoirs were nearly empty when the city council voted to pay Hatfield a fee of $10,000 if he produced enough rain within one year to fill the reservoirs, but not one cent if he failed.

Hatfield, the self-styled "moisture accelerator," had something of a reputation in the rainmaking field, having brought relief to Los Angeles a decade earlier. He set up his paraphernalia on a 20-foot tower atop a hill near the city. On January 1, 1916, he began his procedure, sending a chemical-laden column of smoke skyward as he detonated a series of explosives.

The act must have been even better than usual. A week later the rain commenced and wouldn't stop. By January 19 the reservoirs were full. Soon they began overflowing. Roads, bridges and railroad tracks were washed out. Telephone and telegraph service was disrupted. Thousands of homes were flooded and their occupants evacuated. On January 26 another large storm hit, rupturing the dams at both reservoirs. Twelve people died, and property damage ran into the millions.

Hatfield had to disguise himself and travel under a false name to avoid retribution from the angry townsfolk. Worst of all, the city council refused to pay his fee. He had given them all they had asked for and more, but they were far from pleased. They told him that he'd been hired to save the city, not swamp it.

REAGAN, RONALD; THE WIT AND WISDOM OF

Before a radio broadcast, President Reagan made the following joke into a mike that he didn't realize was open: "My fellow Americans...I've signed legislation that will outlaw Russia forever. We begin bombing in five minutes." According to subsequent reports, Soviet officials were not amused.

In his speech to the 1988 Republican Convention, Reagan punctuated his speech with a quote from John Adams: "Facts are stubborn things." All was going well until, on one pass, the quote came out as "Facts are stupid things."

At a White House reception for the nation's mayors, Reagan went up to a black man, shook his hand and said, "How are you, Mr. Mayor? I'm glad to see you. How are things in your city?" The man Reagan didn't recognize was Samuel Pierce, the Secretary of Housing and Urban Development, who regularly attended Cabinet meetings at which Reagan was present.

LET ME SHOW YOU WHAT HAPPENED...

The Portuguese army courtmartialed a sentry who had shot a 12-year-old boy. The sentry explained that the boy had approached the sentry's position at night, failed to answer a challenge and was shot. During the hearing the incident was reenacted with a civilian playing the part of the boy. He was shot, too.

An American soldier stationed in Panama City, Panama, demonstrated how a friend had been killed when he had accidentally fallen from the fifth-floor balcony of a hotel. Capping the demonstration, the soldier lost his balance and fell to his death.

A cook at a Swiss hotel filed an insurance claim after cutting off his finger on a piece of meat-cutting machinery. The insurance company sent an investigator, who asked if he might be allowed to operate the machine. He cut off a finger as well.

Yooket Paen, a 57-year-old woman in Angthong, Thailand, slipped in mud in her yard and grabbed a live wire to catch her balance, electrocuting herself. That afternoon Yooket Pan, her 52-year-old sister, was showing neighbors how the accident happened. She also grabbed the wire and was killed.

Clement Vallandigham was a highly successful defense lawyer who rarely lost a case. In 1871 he took on the case of Thomas McGehan, who was charged with shooting and killing

Tom Myers in a barroom brawl. Vallandigham planned to argue that Myers had actually shot himself while drawing his pistol. As the lawyer demonstrated how this could have happened, he accidentally shot himself with a gun he hadn't realized was loaded. He died 12 hours later. His client was acquitted.

REINVENTING GOVERNMENT: WE'RE NOT THERE YET

One of Vice President Al Gore's high-profile assignments in the Clinton administration was "Reinventing Government," a catchphrase meant to suggest that ways should be found for government to do its work more efficiently. The report he released, *Creating a Government That Works Better and Costs Less*, was 168 pages long and cost the government $4 each to print. According to the Government Printing Office the per unit cost should have been closer to 90¢. The reason it was so expensive? The report "was produced on the best and most expensive Grade 1 coated paper (high gloss) in multiple ink colors, at Quality Level 2 (on a scale of 1 to 5) on a rush schedule over the Labor Day weekend." The total cost for printing the report was $168,915. It should have been $54,091.

Unfortunately, any useful lessons Al Gore might have drawn from the Government Printing Office's audit came too late for inclusion in his book.

EASY COME, EASY GO

In 1849 Walter Hunt of New York wanted to find some way to pay off a $15 debt. He worked for about three hours, came up with the design for the safety pin and sold the rights to it for $400.

Oil money filled the coffers of Sheik Shakhbut, former leader of Abu Dhabi, but he didn't like to spend any. He kept a fortune in currency in his living quarters. The classic miser stuffs his mattress with cash, but the sheik had so much, the overflow had to be stashed in his dresser, under his bed and in his closets. When he was deposed and his royal residence searched, these hoards of cash were recovered, minus an estimated $2 million that had been shredded by rats.

In July 1886 a penniless prospector named Sors Hariezon found a gold nugget on the ground in South Africa. He had stumbled onto what came to be called the Main Reef, which during the next century produced up to a million kilograms of gold a year, nearly 70% of the production in the Western world, and beside which Johannesburg was built.

Hariezon sold his claim to the spot for £10. He wandered off in search of gold elsewhere, and is rumored to have been eaten by a lion.

Joe Schuster and Jerry Siegel, the two teenagers who created Superman, sold their rights to the character in 1938 for $130, or $65 each.

ROCKEFELLER SEES RED

Who was more capitalistic than the Rockefellers? So, when in the 1930s the family set about constructing its great cathedral of commerce, Rockefeller Center, who better to hire to decorate it with a mural than the unabashed Mexican communist, Diego Rivera? Rivera accepted the job. His somewhat vague pencil sketches passed inspection, and he commenced painting the 63-by-17-foot fresco of American scenes in the main lobby of the building complex.

As he applied the finishing touches, someone spotted a familiar face among a group of workers. Rivera was happy to acknowledge that yes, that was Lenin at the vanguard of the workers' struggle against the exploiting oppressors. And those black and white workers were waving red banners before the unemployed masses. And that deformed, syphilitic girl in the corner represented life under capitalism.

Perhaps the Rockefellers had imagined that their generosity

would buy a little more respect. Although $21,500 had been spent on the mural, Nelson Rockefeller, in charge of the interior decoration on the project, ordered it chipped off the wall.

Years later, perhaps having forgotten the adventure, Rockefeller said, "Art is probably one of the few areas left where there is complete freedom."

THE GLORY THAT WAS ROME

The Renaissance is generally thought of as that period during the fourteenth through sixteenth centuries that Europeans rediscovered and re-created the glory of their Roman and Greek heritage. Actually, it was a time in which they largely trashed it. Despite all its fabled "sackings," Rome wasn't truly done in until the Renaissance. Italians got so excited about ancient Rome that they virtually dismantled the place in order to throw up brand-new buildings to express their reverence for it. Old Saint Peter's Basilica, the oldest, largest and most sacred building in Christendom, dating from the fourth century, was leveled in order to build the new one. Sections of the city that had survived barbarian raids were demolished. Marble columns were swiped from ancient buildings to save the time and expense of cutting new ones. Thousands of classical marble statues were burned in kilns to make lime, needed for plaster. Of course, any chunks of marble from a quarry would do as well, but this stuff was just lying around.

Michelangelo was among those that deplored the practice, to no avail.

ELEANOR ROOSEVELT HONORS FORGOTTEN HEROES

Eleanor Roosevelt was an activist First Lady, the model for others up to and including Hillary Rodham Clinton. During World War II Eleanor Roosevelt traveled tirelessly in an effort to boost morale, meeting with troops and often bringing personal messages from them back home to their families. *Time* magazine reported that, while visiting wounded veterans in a hospital in the South Pacific, she departed from her escorts and burst into a ward full of bedridden soldiers. She shook their hands, hugged them and with great emotion thanked them for the sacrifices they had made in service to their nation, their communities and their loved ones.

At this point her escorts were too embarrassed to inform her that this particular ward was reserved for American soldiers who had contracted venereal diseases.

DISINFORMATION FROM DR. RUTH

In 1986 television and radio's best-known sexual adviser, Dr. Ruth Westheimer, wrote *First Love: A Young People's Guide to Sexual Information*. The book was intended to provide crucial information on sex to a teenaged readership. What would be the most important information a teenager would require, besides how to actually find someone to have sex with? How to avoid pregnancy, of course. Dr. Ruth wrote that it is safe to have intercourse during the week before ovulation. This is exactly backward; it is during this period that a woman is *most* likely to get pregnant. "It's very upsetting," admitted Dr. Ruth. "I don't know how many times I read over that passage, but I just must have not been attentive enough."

First Love had been in the bookstores for three months before the goof was discovered. The publisher, Warner Bros., scrambled to recall the 115,000 copies already in distribution and put out a corrected edition with a redesigned cover. "The first book came out in white," said Dr. Ruth. "But I made a mistake, I blushed, now it's red."

No word on how many tykes resulted from the typo.

RESCUE DOG FACES EARLY RETIREMENT

A Saint Bernard named Bruno was a member of the mountain rescue team in the village of Valchiusella in the northern Italian Alps. Whether he could be described as a "valued" member is another story. Whenever the search team set out, Bruno always raced ahead, often becoming lost himself. On one occasion in 1980 a second search party had to be sent out to rescue Bruno long after the first rescue party had accomplished its mission and returned to the village. That was the eighth time in his two-year career that Bruno had had to be rescued, and as a result he was granted early retirement.

FROM THE ANNALS OF IRRELEVANT RESEARCH: THE HUMAN CAPACITY FOR GAS

Shortly after the invention of the X-ray in 1895, Dr. Nicholas Senn, professor of surgery at Rush Medical College in Chicago, theorized that better pictures of the human intestine would be possible if it were first inflated with some sort of gas. To test his theory, Senn inserted a rubber tube up his own rectum and pumped helium into his nether regions. Though the theory that this would improve X-ray images did not pan out, Senn was able to establish that the human bowel has a capacity of 5 imperial gallons, a fact that no additional study has ever endeavored to disprove, and for which no practical application has ever been found. It does, however, sound like the sort of information that fraternity boys could find some use for.

INDIANS DEMAND FAT-FREE AMMO

The Sepoy Rebellion was a widespread, violent uprising against British rule eight decades after it had been imposed on India. Tens of thousands, both British and Indian, lost their lives. Though the rebellion was fueled by long-standing resentments, the spark that set it off was an utterly thoughtless act of the British.

In 1857 223,000 Indian troops in British regiments were issued a new weapon, the Enfield rifle, to replace the old Brown Bess musket that had been in use since the time of the American Revolution. The Enfield was lighter and had far greater range and accuracy. To load it, the soldier bit the end off a greased paper cartridge, poured the powder down the barrel, then rammed the bullet home. British officers insisted that Indian troops follow the procedure exactly as it had been established. Unfortunately, the grease on the cartridges came either from beef or pork fat—one sacred to Hindus, the other taboo. The Indians refused to bite the cartridges and, after being disciplined, began the bloody rebellion in protest.

SERGEANT YORK ROLLS OVER IN HIS GRAVE

During the 1980s the Pentagon got a significant boost in its credit limit. It went a little wild, paying $110 apiece for electri-

cal diodes that were available 10 for 99¢ at Radio Shack, $1,676 for a 10-foot aluminum ladder and $18,000 for a sofa for an officers' wardroom on a navy destroyer. Then there was the air force's $7,000 coffeemaker for installation on aircraft, whose cost was justified by the fact that it was guaranteed to survive a crash that would kill the entire crew. This is all nickel-and-dime stuff; when the military really wants to waste money, it procures a new weapons system.

At the end of the 1970s the army decided it needed a self-propelled antiaircraft gun that could protect tanks and infantry from attack by low-flying planes and helicopters. The weapons system was initially called DIVAD—for Division Air Defense—but soon acquired the name Sergeant York, for the World War I hero. The army planned to buy 600 of them at $4.8 billion.

Once the Sergeant Yorks began rolling off the assembly lines, one was demonstrated before high-ranking military personnel and defense contractors. The demonstration was not a success. Instead of locking on to the intended target, the guns swiveled and came to rest aimed directly at the reviewing stand, causing the top brass to hit the dirt. At a later test, the radar failed to identify the whirling blades of an approaching helicopter, opting instead for the whirling blades of the exhaust fan in a nearby latrine. Even when the test helicopter's rotors were outfitted with special reflectors to assist the Sergeant York's radar—a modification that Warsaw Pact countries were unlikely to adopt—it still failed to find it.

It had other problems. It wouldn't start when it was cold outside and overheated when it was hot. It was too slow to keep up with the tanks it was supposed to protect. Its range of 2 1/2 miles was a mile less than its specifications had called for. It had trouble hitting anything that didn't fly in a perfectly straight line.

The Sergeant York program was canceled in 1985 after $1.8 billion had already been spent. The 65 units delivered to the army were dismantled and sold for scrap.

A historical aside: In World War I, the infantry company of Sergeant Alvin C. York was pinned down and being cut to pieces by enemy machine gunfire. York, a backwoodsman from Tennessee, used his Enfield rifle to shoot the German machine gunners the instant they raised their heads above the trenches, killing 18. When the Germans mounted a bayonet charge against him, he coolly took down all seven with the seven rounds in his Colt .45 automatic. He probably would have wanted a serious talk with the Pentagon desk-jockey who attached his name to this thing.

SEWARD'S FOLLY GETS LAST LAUGH

Russia had begun colonizing Alaska in the 1780s, but by the mid-nineteenth century many Americans and Canadians had settled there as well. America negotiated with Russia to purchase the territory, and on March 30, 1867, Czar Alexander II accepted a payment of $7.3 million, about 2¢ an acre. William Seward, the U.S. secretary of state who made the purchase, was ridiculed for buying a frozen wasteland, and was almost forced to resign. Alaska was called "Seward's Folly," "Walrussia" and "Icebergia."

What appeared to be a great American blunder was seen to be a Russian one 30 years later, when gold was discovered in the Klondike. A century after the purchase, rich oil fields were discovered on Alaska's North Slope.

THE FRUIT THAT FOILED THE SEYCHELLES OP

Colonel "Mad" Mike Hoare became a legend among mercenaries in the 1960s for his exploits during the war in the Belgian Congo (now Zaire). He served as a technical adviser on the film *The Wild Geese*, and the character played by Richard Burton was based on him. Hoare retired to a small town in South Africa, but heads of state throughout Africa liked to be kept informed of his activities, suspecting that he had not entirely withdrawn from contract work. They were right.

In 1981 Hoare became involved in a plot to overthrow the leftist military regime that ruled the Seychelles, an 89-island archipelago in the western Indian Ocean.

Hoare assembled a 52-man team of mercenary soldiers that he believed would be sufficient to seize Victoria, the capital city. In November 1981 five members of the team went in to handle the advance work. Shortly afterward the remaining 47 soldiers entered by passenger aircraft, posing as a vacationing rugby team called AOFB, for Ancient Order of Foam Blowers. Customs inspection at the Seychelles Airport was run on the honor system, so the mercs smuggled in their AK-47s in golf bags and suitcases.

Everything was going exactly as planned until one of the mercs, Johan Fritz, evidently decided that the violent overthrow of a government was one thing, but the violation of agricultural import regulations quite another. He entered the voluntary customs inspection line because he was carrying several litchi fruits, which he was concerned might be proscribed. The customs inspector examining his bag discovered his AK-47. The inspector shouted for security and all hell broke loose. One of the other mercs was heard to mutter, "Lovely, lovely," as he pulled out his gun and joined the ensuing fracas. Some members of the group were captured, while others who hijacked a plane back to South Africa were arrested upon their arrival.

Note to aspiring mercenaries: If fruit smuggling makes you nervous, consider another line of work.

THE NIGHTMARE OF THE 1957 KENTUCKY DERBY

Willie Shoemaker was the winningest jockey in history, and that's why Texas oilman Ralph Lowe hired him to ride his colt, Gallant Man, in the 1957 Kentucky Derby. Gallant Man had a good chance at winning the roses, and Lowe wanted a rider who could bring out the horse's best. Nevertheless, the day before the race, Lowe told Shoemaker about a strange nightmare he had had. He had dreamed that Gallant Man was winning the Derby, but Shoemaker misjudged the 16th pole for the finish line and stood up in his stirrups, losing the race. Shoemaker laughed and reassured Lowe that such a thing could never happen.

The next day it did happen. Coming around the final turn on the outside, Shoemaker made his move. Gallant Man moved from seventh place to the lead in the last quarter mile. When he galloped past the 16th pole, Shoemaker stood triumphantly in his stirrups, just as in Lowe's nightmare. By standing up he slowed Gallant Man enough that he lost by a nose to Iron Liege. A mortified Shoemaker was suspended for 15 days, and as a result Lowe, who stood by him, didn't enter Gallant Man in the Preakness. Later, at the Belmont,

Shoemaker rode the colt to a eight-length win, which convinced him that Gallant Man could have been a Triple Crown winner but for his stupid blunder.

Shoemaker did point out that the finish line at Churchill Downs is a 16th of a mile farther toward the first turn than at any other track in the country. He also said, "I know it was a character-builder for me. It taught me humility. And that's not a bad lesson for anyone."

SKYDIVER FILMS FINAL JUMP

Ivan Lester McQuire, the owner and chief instructor of a skydiving school in North Carolina, wanted to make a promotional commercial. He took his best students aloft for a jump, and equipped himself with video equipment in order to record the event. He taped shots of the students inside the plane, then leapt out of the hatchway himself and filmed them performing aerial stunts before popping their chutes. At about that point McQuire evidently realized he had forgotten to put on his own parachute. His arms can be seen flailing at the sides of the frame as the ground approaches faster and faster. Though McQuire did not survive the skydiving session, his tape did. It has been aired on a Japanese version of "funniest home videos."

THE SMELL-O-METER

During the Vietnam War the American military sometimes felt as if it were hunting moths with a shotgun. It had overwhelming force at its disposal, but the prey was maddeningly elusive.

To help it locate the enemy, U.S. Army scientists invented an electronic "Smell-O-Meter." This sensitive device was intended to detect the body odor of the Vietnamese, distinctive because of the pungent *nuoc mam* fish sauce they ate on their rice. Placed along the Ho Chi Minh Trail, the path by which the North Vietnamese infiltrated the south, the Smell-O-Meters would alert U.S. forces to their movements. The expensive and sophisticated detection devices were installed but quickly neutralized. The North Vietnamese hung buckets of urine in trees along the trail, causing the Smell-O-Meter to give a constant reading of no value whatsoever.

SON TAY MISSION A COMPLETE SUCCESS, BUT...

In early 1970, with the Vietnam War winding down, a dramatic plan was hatched to rescue some 60 American POWs held at the Son Tay prison camp just 23 miles from Hanoi. Special Forces Lieutenant Colonel Arthur "Bull" Simons was chosen to organize and lead the operation. He picked 59 elite troops from the Special Operations Group and Green Berets, and for months the team trained nightly on a full-scale mock-up of the Son Tay camp at the Elgin Air Force Base in Florida. The mock-up was constructed in such a way that it could be disassembled during daylight hours to escape detection from the twice-daily over-flights of Soviet spy satellites.

The raid was launched on November 20, 1970. A heavy air campaign was used as a diversion to keep North Vietnamese anti-aircraft gunners busy while the commandos infiltrated by helicopter. At Son Tay they met stiff resistance, and killed an estimated 100 to 200 of the enemy while suffering no more serious injury among their own men than a broken ankle.

The Son Tay raid had been meticulously planned and was flawlessly executed. There was only one problem: There were no POWs to be rescued. The prison had been closed three months earlier, and the intelligence reports on which the raid was based had not been updated for six months.

BUZZING RED SQUARE

The United States spent tens of billions of dollars in the 1980s developing military aircraft capable of getting past the air defense system of the USSR, such as the low-flying B-1 bomber and the radar-invisible B-2 Stealth. Little did we know that a single-engine Cessna was the ticket.

On May 28, 1987, Mathias Rust, a 19-year-old West German, flew from Helsinki to Moscow in his Cessna 172 across 500 miles of what was supposed to be the most heavily defended air space on Earth. He circled Red Square and buzzed the Kremlin before landing in front of St. Basil's Cathedral. Rust announced he was trying to promote world peace.

The Soviet Union, which gives high priority to its border defenses, was not amused by the ease with which Rust penetrated undetected to the heart of Moscow. A string of top-ranking military officials lost their jobs, and Rust was sentenced to four years in a labor camp. Perhaps it wouldn't have been so embarrassing if Rust hadn't happened to fly into Moscow on the annual celebration of "Border Guards Day."

SOVIET CITIZEN SEEKS PROTECTION

During the years of the Cold War and the Iron Curtain, it was not uncommon for Soviets given the rare opportunity to travel to take the earliest opportunity to defect.

In the 1980s a young Russian couple walked into a duty-free shop at the Shannon International Airport in Ireland, and the man told the clerk, in broken English, that they needed "protection." Figuring that he was requesting political asylum, the clerk summoned airport officials who immediately put the couple under protective custody. After further consultation it turned out that the man was only trying to purchase some condoms.

THE SPY WHO LOST THE WAR

Carl Hans Lody, a German spy in England during World War I, uncovered an extremely important piece of classified information. Evidently there were large numbers of Russian troops stationed in England who were going to be sent to France. Lody's intelligence coup was based on reports of troop trains traveling with all the window blinds drawn; one of his contacts had asked a soldier where he was from, and was told "Russia."

After Lody wired his report, the German army held back two divisions from the front to meet the Russian threat. That decision may have cost it the Battle of the Marne.

Lody's reports, it turned out, had been somewhat in error. The troop trains he saw carried Scottish soldiers, not Russian. The blinds were closed not for secrecy but so that the troops could sleep. The regiment was from Ross Shire, which sounded to his contact like "Russia."

Lody became known as "the spy who lost the war."

A STATUE FOR JOSÉ OLMEDO

The city of Guayaquil, Ecuador, wished to honor the national poet, José Olmedo, with a statue. Ecuador is a poor country, however, and after a panel found out how much it would cost to commission a sculptor, it submitted an alternate plan that was accepted. It bought a statue of the English poet Lord Byron from a London junk dealer, changed the nameplate and erected it in Olmedo's honor.

STINGERS TO AFGHANISTAN AND BACK AGAIN

During the Soviet occupation of Afghanistan, the CIA funneled about a thousand sophisticated shoulder-fired, surface-to-air missiles ("Stingers") to the Afghan rebels, who made good use of them. Heavy losses of expensive attack helicopters helped persuade the USSR that occupying Afghanistan was not worth the trouble.

Since the end of the war Congress has had to authorize more than $65 million for the CIA to buy back remaining stocks of the Stingers. There is considerable concern that the Afghans will sell them to terrorists, and some of the Stingers have already shown up in Iran and North Korea.

The Stingers, which were given to the Afghan rebels for free, originally cost the U.S. government $35,000 each from General Dynamics. The Afghans are now demanding $100,000 apiece for their return.

Never expect gratitude.

A BRIDGE WITH BOUNCE: TACOMA NARROWS BRIDGE

On July 1, 1940, the ribbon was cut on the Tacoma Narrows Bridge across Washington's Puget Sound. It had cost $6.5 million to build, and at 2,800 feet was the third longest suspension bridge in the world at that time. Suspension bridge technology was considered to have been perfected, with the Golden Gate and George Washington bridges in service for years. However, a problem immediately became obvious with the Tacoma Narrows Bridge: In high winds the span displayed an alarming flexibility, with wavelike motions passing between its towers. Engineers later determined that the bridge had been designed without accounting for aerodynamic effects. The narrow, two-lane roadway gave the span too much flexibility, and there were other structural weaknesses as well.

The Tacoma Narrows Bridge was popular with motorists who drove across just to experience its peculiar undulations. Four months after "Galloping Gertie" opened, the fun ended. On November 7, a 42-mile-per-hour wind set up oscillations that escalated rapidly until several of the suspenders were torn lose. After that the span broke apart and tumbled into the water below. Fortunately, the bridge had been closed in time and only one abandoned car remained on it.

There is film footage of the breakup and it was recently used in a prize-winning TV ad. The camera closes in on that one car in the middle of the rocking and rolling bridge to show that the driver inside is listening to his Pioneer stereo. He says, "Sorry," switches it off, and the bridge returns to normal.

A properly designed bridge was opened in 1952, erected upon the still-standing piers of the original.

A *TITANIC* ERROR

On April 14, 1912, two days after setting out on her maiden voyage, the *Titanic* sank her way onto the list of the world's greatest blunders. The tragic story involved a series of mistakes that together wove a tapestry of disaster. Captain Edward J. Smith has been faulted for ignoring warnings of icebergs and maintaining full speed. Opprobrium is also heaped on Captain Stanley Lord of the *Californian*, who didn't respond to the

Titanic's distress rockets and radio calls. Ironically though, a large measure of blame belongs not to someone who didn't do his job, but to two who did their jobs conscientiously. When Seaman Frederick Fleet, in the crow's nest, spotted the iceberg dead ahead and gave the alarm, First Officer Murdoch, on the bridge, gave the order "Hard a-starboard." Ironically, if the iceberg had not been spotted and the *Titanic* had hit it dead on, disaster would have been averted. There would have been injuries and perhaps even deaths, but at most two of the ship's 16 watertight compartments would have been flooded, a situation that she was designed to survive. As it was, the grazing pass opened a gash in the ship's side 300 feet long, flooding six compartments and assuring her doom.

RAISE THE TITANIC! ALSO GOES DOWN

The bad luck of the *Titanic* did not end with its sinking. A little of it seemed to rub off on *Raise the Titanic!*, a film based on the Clive Cussler bestseller. The 1980 British-made film cost $40 million, considerably more than the *Titanic* itself, but like that fabled ship went quickly under, earning only $7 million. Among its extravagances was $350,000 spent on an extremely accurate 55-foot model of the ship, which turned out to be too large to fit into the studio tank in which most of the movie would be filmed. To solve the problem, a larger tank was built—at a cost of a mere $6 million.

As Lord Lew Grade, the film's producer, ruefully told his shareholders, "Raise the *Titanic*...it would have been cheaper to lower the Atlantic."

TOILETS, ACCIDENTS INVOLVING

Convicted murderer Michael Anderson Godwin had successfully avoided the electric chair through years of appeals. In 1989, sitting on a steel toilet seat in his cell while attempting to repair a set of headphones, he accidentally electrocuted himself.

The Public Works Department of Beatrice, Nebraska, discovered that a $12,000 high-pressure sewer-cleaning system it had installed could force water in toilets to shoot out as high as the ceiling. A spokesman, questioned about the engineering error, explained, "It's just one of those things."

An exploding toilet in Arnhem, Netherlands, had police baffled. For the second time in two years Miriam Smonk's toilet blew off the floor. "It really keeps blowing up into a thousand pieces," Smonk stated. "My son was almost hit by a piece that flew out the door."

After an investigation, the Environmental Inspection Authority offered its opinion that the explosions were caused by volatile solvents released into the sewers. Commenting on the attention her plumbing problem has drawn, Mrs. Smonk said, "I feel famous."

It all started with a cockroach in a Tel Aviv apartment, according to a story in the *Jerusalem Post*. After the unidentified housewife stomped it, she threw it in the toilet but still it refused to die. To finish it off she emptied an entire can of bug spray into the toilet bowl.

Minutes later her husband went into the bathroom, sat down and smoked a cigarette. Still seated, he dropped the still-burning butt into the bowl, which caused the insecticide fumes to ignite in a flash, burning his own butt. His wife called for an ambulance.

While the ambulance crew carried him down the stairs on a stretcher, he explained what had happened. The paramedics began laughing so hard that they dropped him, breaking two of his ribs.

FAILURES TO COMMUNICATE

Workers in San Jose, California, had to remove a 30-foot banner in front of the public library. It had been intended to read, in the Tagalog language of the Philippines, "You Are Welcome." Unfortunately, it read "You Are Circumcised."

The great explorer Captain Cook gave the *kangaroo* its name. Upon his arrival in Australia in 1770, he asked the aborigines what they called the strange-looking animals. "Kangaroo," they answered, which Cook recorded in his ship's log as the name for the beast. In the Australian aborigines' language, kangaroo means "I don't know."

A Spanish explorer christened Mexico's Yucatan peninsula when he landed there early in the sixteenth century. He asked the Indians what they called their land, and they replied "Yucatan," which in their language means "What do you want?"

TREASURE SHIP YIELDS SURPRISING SALVAGE

In 1983, when an Icelandic salvage company announced that it had located the sunken remains of the *Wapen Van Amsterdam*, a Dutch treasure ship that went down in 1667 with 40 crates of gold and 4 tons of uncut diamonds aboard, gold fever raged. The government of Iceland invested millions of dollars in the raising of the wreck, which was well preserved in the frigid North Atlantic waters off its coast. Special equipment was brought in that could make tunnels beneath the hulk, through which cables could be strung. When enough cable had been fitted to raise the ship on a supporting sling, Icelanders awaited the raising with barely contained excitement. Government officials were on hand for the event. The salvage crew put their winches into action. The crowd waited impatiently during the painfully slow process and exuberantly cheered when at last the hulk of a wooden ship broke through the surface.

It was the hulk of a German trawler that had sunk in 1903. Its precious cargo: herring.

TREASURES LOST

A rare and valuable collection of first edition plays was amassed by John Warburton (1682-1759). He owned 58, including most of the works of Shakespeare. Warburton returned home one day to discover that the size of his collection had been significantly reduced. A servant in his house, Betsy Baker, had used 55 of the plays to kindle a fire in the kitchen stove and as pie bottoms. The three that remained are now held by the British Museum.

In one of the most important archaeological finds of all time, a skull of Peking man was unearthed in China in 1929. The skull was carefully packaged to be shipped out of the country for safekeeping when the Japanese invaded. When the package was opened in Shanghai, though, it was empty—the priceless skull had been stolen in transit. It is believed that it was stolen by black marketeers, who ground the skull into fine powder for sale as an aphrodisiac.

In 1922 Ernest Hemingway was working in Switzerland as a

correspondent. His first wife, Hadley, decided to join him there for Christmas. To surprise him she brought along all his old manuscripts, including their carbon copies. The valise containing them was stolen at the Paris railroad station. The contents included Hemingway's untitled first novel and several unpublished short stories.

Hemingway soon remarried.

The Soviet cellist Agustinas Vassiliauskas was mounting the podium for the third time to receive the audience's thunderous ovation after his performance at the 1980 Kuhmo Music Festival when he tripped and fell, smashing his priceless 300-year-old Ruggieri cello beyond repair.

A youth group cleaning up graffiti in the Mayrieres Cave near Brunquiel in southwest France accidentally wiped away part of a 15,000-year-old cave painting.

Rain forests are home to numerous rare species of plant life, some of which have as-yet unknown medicinal potential. In 1987, exploring a Malaysian rain forest, University of Illinois plant researcher D. D. Soejarto discovered an unfamiliar species of tree from which he extracted a sample of sap. Some years later, working with the sap in his laboratory, he developed a compound that seemed to inhibit the growth of the AIDS virus. Soejarto returned to Malaysia in 1992 to extract more sap from the tree and to obtain its seeds, only to find that it had been cut down for lumber.

CONSPICUOUS FAILURES OF THE TRUTH-IN-PACKAGING LAW

A Catholic girls' school in St. Louis, Missouri, ordered 25 copies of the *Joy of Cooking* from a book distributor in 1974. The distributor mistakenly shipped them 25 copies of *The Joy of Sex*. Strangely enough, the school did not notify the distributor of the error and promptly paid its bill.

Some shoppers who opened their 1982 Montgomery Wards' catalog found a *Playboy* centerfold in the middle. A Montgomery

Ward spokesman explained that the catalog and the men's magazine were printed in the same plant, and that the mixup occurred as a result of "an employee prank."

Lawrence Welk fans who bought his 1987 *Polka Party* album got an altogether different listening experience. The record contained the rock soundtrack to *Sid and Nancy*, the raunchy movie about former Sex Pistol Sid Vicious. About 10,000 albums were mislabeled at the factory, explained a spokeswoman for the Welk Music Group, who had to field numerous calls from startled senior citizens.

A new edition of *Captain Kidd's Cat*, a 1991 children's book about the adventures of the pirate's pet, was found to include a 32 page section from a book on sadomasochistic homosexual relationships.

TROUBLE WITH TULIPS

Many investors subscribe to the "bigger fool theory," which holds that it doesn't matter what you spend on a commodity as long as you can count on there being a bigger fool coming after you who will pay even more. However, the supply of fools is limited, and sometimes you turn out to be the biggest one of all. The bigger fool theory has been behind booms and busts in real estate, the stock market, precious metals and, in seventeenth-century Holland, tulip bulbs.

Tulips were introduced into Holland in the late 1500s, at a time when the nation was becoming rich through trade. The flower was featured in the gardens of the rich, and soon became popular with the bourgeoisie. Tulip breeders found that the plant's frequent mutations produced occasional blossoms of striking beauty. These became highly sought after, and the value of their bulbs was driven up. In 1634 a speculative frenzy began, with prices for tulip bulbs being bid to dizzying heights. A single bulb for the rare Semper Augustus, a red-and-white-striped blossom with a blue-tinted base, sold for as much as 5,500 florins—the equivalent of 8 pounds of gold. During the period of tulipmania, common sense seemed to be suspended as everyone from noblemen to chimney sweeps hurried to cultivate a patch of land with tulips. The government tried to discourage the wild speculation, and publications ridiculed those who traded their fortunes for 40 or 50 bulbs, but as long as enormous profits were being made it was hard to quench the fever. The price of bulbs grew so high that their value was reckoned in fractions, so that ordinary investors could afford to get a foot in the market. The rich investor disdained actual bulbs for what was called the "wind trade"—futures contracts on bulbs that were not yet grown but which the investor agreed to purchase at a set price.

MacKay's *Extraordinary Popular Delusions and the Madness of Crowds* describes a blunder that occurred at the height of the frenzy. A ship returned from the Middle East, and a sailor was sent into town to tell the wealthy merchant who had sponsored the voyage that his goods had arrived safely. The happy merchant rewarded the sailor with a fine smoked herring for his breakfast. The sailor, liking a bit of sliced onion with his fish, saw what appeared to be a bulb on the merchant's desk, and figured the rich man wouldn't begrudge him it. He took his breakfast back to the dock and was enjoying it until the flustered minions of the merchant finally located him. The sailor, who had been out of his native land during the period of the tulipmania, had no idea that the "onion" he'd eaten was a *Semper Augustus*, whose value could have provisioned a shipload of seamen for a month. The unfortunate sailor was imprisoned for his crime.

Such madness cannot sustain itself for long, and in February 1637 the supply of "bigger fools" ran out. The price of bulbs plummeted, and investors refused to honor the futures contracts they had signed for bulbs now worth a tiny fraction of what they had agreed to pay for them. These cases went to court, where they were ruled to be gambling debts, unenforceable by law.

LEAVE IT TO THE GOVERNMENT

In the 1960s, the U.S. government shipped a 139-year supply of condoms to Thailand as part of an Agency for International Development package. The condoms had a shelf life of five to 10 years.

In 1981 the Department of Agriculture attempted to save money on government-subsidized school lunches by classifying ketchup and relish as vegetables, and sunflower seeds as meat. The Reagan administration later withdrew the plan due to widespread derision.

Taxpayers who go to the IRS with tax questions may not always receive the right answers. In fact, according to the General Accounting Office, 31% of the IRS' written responses to taxpayer inquiries contain errors, and another 16% of those responses are incomplete or unclear.

A small typing error brought an army clerk at Fort Carson, Colorado, an unexpectedly large package. Requisitioning a $6.04 lightbulb, the clerk thought he had typed the correct code number into his computer, #2040-00-368-4972, but had actually sent in a request for item #2040-00-368-4772. A week later the clerk received a $28,000, 14,500-pound battleship anchor. No one at the Naval Supply Center had thought to ask what a base in the middle of Colorado would want with a 7-ton anchor. Novelty paperweight, perhaps?

The Georgia State Game Commission spent a considerable amount of time debating the pros and cons of regulating alligator rides before someone realized that they were victims of a typographical error. At that point the debate turned to the intended topic, the regulation of alligator *hides*.

During the military operation in Panama, Pentagon spokesmen claimed to have found 50 kilograms of cocaine in General Noriega's refrigerator intended for distribution. They later admitted that it was actually 50 kilograms of cornmeal intended for making tamales.

To promote its toy safety campaign, the Consumer Products Safety Commission made up 80,000 buttons in time for Christmas, 1974. The buttons read "For Kids' Sakes, Think Toy Safety."

The buttons had to be immediately withdrawn. It was discovered that they had sharp edges, pins that came off easily and which a child could swallow and were painted with a lead-based pigment.

A program in which employees of the Tennessee Valley Authority were rewarded for suggestions that saved the utility money had to be ended in 1988. Though 46 suggestions had been implemented that led to $580,000 in savings, it cost $700,000 to administer the program.

UNITED ARTISTS LEAVES THROUGH *HEAVEN'S GATE*

After writer-director Michael Cimino won five Academy Awards in 1979 for *The Deer Hunter*, executives at United Artists patted themselves on the back for having been shrewd enough to back his next project, *Heaven's Gate*. Two years later they were kicking themselves somewhere else. Though budgeted at $11.6 million, cost overruns brought the gargantuan epic Western in at a staggering $45 million, the most ever spent on a film at that time. How had Cimino managed to run up that kind of expense on a film with no major stars and no special effects? Through a rampant profligacy that made Hollywood history. A few examples:

- A Western town was built at his Montana location, but the width of the street "didn't look right" to Cimino. Both sides of the street were torn down and built again, 3 feet back. Cimino rejected a suggestion that one side of the street be left alone and the other moved back 6 feet to save half the money.

- Cimino insisted that the crew be on call 12 to 18 hours a day, seven days a week, in case he had a flash of genius. With overtime and penalties, this boosted the average weekly wage of the unionized workers from $1,000 to $5,000. To the crew, *Heaven's Gate* became known as "The Montana Gold Rush."

- An unprecedented 1.5 million feet of film was shot. (Films average less than 100,000 feet.) Cimino held a celebration when he'd surpassed Coppola's million-foot record on Apocalypse Now. He shot 30 separate takes of a land baron mooning a crowd, an image that sums up the whole venture. He also printed an unparalleled percentage of what he shot, going into the editing booth with 500 hours.

It might have been worth it if the resulting 3-hour-and-39-minute western was great art, but when Heaven's Gate premiered in New York on November 18, 1980, the critics launched their ripest tomatoes:

"*Heaven's Gate* is something quite rare in movies these days—an unqualified disaster," wrote Vincent Canby in the *New York Times*.

"...it's a movie you want to deface; you want to draw mustaches on it..." wrote Pauline Kael in the *New Yorker*.

"It's like *Gone with the Wind*—without the wind," said one critic.

United Artists, with over $40 million invested, quickly withdrew *Heaven's Gate* to try to salvage it. On April 23, after months of re-editing, a 2-hour-and-28-minute version was rereleased. During its first week in 810 theaters, it grossed only $1.3 million, an average of $500 a night per theater, barely enough to pay for the film cans to transport the print. At this point, with promotional expenses and debt service, *Heaven's Gate* would have had to gross $140 million just to break even, and unless everyone in America decided they had to see for themselves just how bad it was, that wasn't going to happen.

The movie sunk the studio, which was sold off to MGM, and fingers were pointed in every direction. Cimino, of course, blamed the American public for being unworthy of his genius. More objective analysts cite one inexplicable error that United Artists made. It hired Joann Carelli as line producer, responsible for making sure that the production stayed within its budget. It did this although it knew that Carelli, whose only credit was as a consultant on *The Deer Hunter*, was Cimino's girlfriend.

THE USSR: AHEAD OF ALL NATIONS FOR 61 YEARS

For most of the twentieth century the Soviet Union felt it was ahead of the decadent West, and it turned out to be a tragic mistake. We are not referring to communism here, but to the fact that in 1991 Soviet officials revealed that their nation's clocks had been wrong for 61 years. In the spring of 1930 clocks were set ahead one hour for daylight savings time. That fall Stalin forgot to tell everyone to set their clocks back, and no one had the temerity to do so without explicit orders. So in the spring of 1931, when the clocks were again set ahead, an hour was lost that was never recovered.

In 1991, with communism in disgrace, the Soviet government was at last willing to admit its errors and try to rectify them. Citizens did not set their clocks forward that spring, but set them back in the fall.

VASA MATTER?

In the early seventeenth century, during the Thirty Years War, King Gustavus II Adolphus of Sweden ordered that the world's largest warship be constructed as the flagship of his navy. The *Vasa* was designed along the lines of the great warships of England and the Netherlands. She carried 500 sailors and soldiers, and 64 cannon in two tiers along her 204-foot hull. Her three masts soared 165 feet above her keel, and with 13,000 square feet of sail she was expected to make 11 knots in a good wind. She was lavishly covered with more than 1,000 sculpted and gilded decorations. Her size and grandeur would proclaim the power and wealth of the Swedish monarch throughout the Baltic.

The *Vasa* set out on her maiden voyage on Sunday, August 10, 1628, from Stockholm harbor, in front of the royal palace. High court and military dignitaries were aboard, and crowds cheered from the quay. Sunlight glinted off her figurehead, a noble lion, snarling ferociously. Sculpted on the underside of each gunport cover was a golden lion against a blood-red background. These were visible to the crowds as the gunports were all open, with a polished bronze cannon poking out from each. The *Vasa* headed out of the harbor, her sails filled by a gentle breeze, her blue-and-yellow Swedish pennants flapping atop her masts. She fired a two-gun salute of departure.

Suddenly the wind blew harder. The *Vasa* heeled. Water poured into her lower gunports, only a yard above the waterline. Within minutes the *Vasa* settled into the 110-foot depths of the harbor. Her blue pennants remained above the Baltic, still proudly flapping atop the masts, at a slightly drunken angle.

BATON TWIRLERS ON THE RAMPAGE

The Ventura Baton Twirling Troupe of Ventura, California, was famous for the height and range of its baton tosses. One performance in the late 1960s will be hard to surpass, however. During the Independence Day parade, one twirler tossed his metal baton up into power lines. The resulting short circuit blacked out a 10-block section of the town, knocked out the local radio station and started a grass fire.

"They were on form," remarked the mayor.

LITTLE-KNOWN TRAGEDIES OF THE VIETNAM WAR

The *St. Louis Post-Dispatch* carried the following wire service story during the Vietnam War:

SAIGON, South Viet Nam, June 7—Nguyen Van Teo, an employee of the United States Army in Saigon, requested sick leave. His reasons:

"(1) When I arrived at building T-1640 to fix it, I found that the rains had dislodged a large number of tiles on the roof. So I rigged up a beam with a pulley at the top of the building and hoisted up a couple barrels of tile.

"(2) When I fixed the building there was a lot of the tile left over. I hoisted the barrel back up again and secured the line at the bottom and then went up and filled the barrel with the extra tile. Then I went down to the bottom and cast off the line.

"(3) Unfortunately the barrel of tile was heavier than I was and before I knew what was happening the barrel started down and I started up. I decided to hang on, and halfway up met the barrel which was coming down, and received a severe blow on the shoulder.

"(4) I then continued to the top, banging my head on the beam and getting my fingers jammed in the pulley. When the barrel hit the ground it burst its bottom, allowing all the tile to spill out. I was now heavier than the barrel and started down again at a high speed.

"(5) Halfway down I met the barrel coming up, and received severe injuries on my shin. When I hit the ground I landed on the tile, getting several painful cuts from the sharp edges.

"(6) At this point I must have lost my presence of mind because I let go of the line. The barrel then came down giving me another heavy blow on the head and putting me in the hospital.

"I respectfully ask for sick leave."

WASHINGTON'S DIGNITY

In the intoxicating euphoria of democracy during the Constitutional Convention, Gouverneur Morris pronounced himself the equal of any man, whereupon Alexander Hamilton challenged him to a little wager. No one was held in greater awe than General Washington; if Morris would treat him in a familiar manner, Hamilton promised to buy him a dinner with wine. Morris accepted the wager, walked up to Washington and slapped him on the back. In return he got a look that chilled him to the bone. He later ruefully observed that he had never lost as much on a wager as he had in the winning of that one.

The famous portrait artist Gilbert Stuart also collided with Washington's frosty reserve. Stuart had been the preeminent portraitist for the European nobility, who enjoyed what has been described as the "showy and outrageous" chitchat with which he diverted his subjects. Washington was not amused by Gilbert's flippant manner. In an attempt to get Washington to let down his guard, Stuart said, "Now, sir, you must let me forget that you are General Washington and I am Stuart the painter." Though Washington intended no insult, he stung the painter with his reply: "Mr. Stuart need never feel the need for forgetting who he is and who General Washington is." It is not wise to anger the man who will portray you for posterity, especially a man as petty and vindictive as Stuart. For most of his adult life Washington had been troubled by ill-fitting dentures, which distorted his lips. Stuart had him remove the false teeth, and pad the space behind his lower lip with cotton. Stuart then rendered Washington's mouth in the unattractive manner—some have said it looks like a mail slot—that has defined the way most people visualize our first president.

WATERGATE: A THIRD–RATE BURGLARY IF THERE EVER WAS ONE

The Watergate burglary on June 17, 1972, in which Nixon operatives attempted to bug Democratic National Committee (DNC) headquarters at the Watergate office complex, ultimately brought down the Nixon administration. When it was discovered, Press Secretary Ron Ziegler dismissed it as a "third-rate burglary," which outraged those who saw it as a threat to the integrity of our political system. However, G. Gordon Liddy's own account of the operation in his autobiography, *Will*, makes "third rate" sound like excessive praise.

The first attempt was on May 26, 1972. The "plumbers," Nixon's clandestine crew, rented a banquet hall in the Watergate building. They planned to hang around until after DNC headquarters closed, and then slip upstairs past the security guards. However, Democratic staffers worked late that night and the break-in could not be performed. Members of the team got locked in the banquet room, where they had to spend the night hiding from guards in a liquor cabinet. The next day Howard Hunt, rejoining Liddy, commented that although Liddy liked scotch, he'd be advised not to order it at the Watergate Hotel. Liddy asked why, and Hunt explained that while hiding in the liquor cabinet he'd had to take a leak. The only handy receptacle was a nearly empty bottle of Johnny Walker Red, which he'd left full.

The following night, entry was once again attempted. Gonzalez, one of the Cubans on the team, "worked long and hard" trying to pick the lock on the door, without success. He complained he had left his good lock-picking tools in Miami and went back to get them.

G. Gordon Liddy

The following night, May 28, equipped with the proper tools, the team entered the DNC offices and planted their electronic bugs. Mission accomplished—or so it seemed. The main bug, which had cost $30,000 and was supposed to pick up all conversation in the room, seemed not to be working. A second entry was planned to repair the bug, as well as to photograph secret files.

One of the plumbers, former FBI agent James McCord, put a strip of electrical tape over the lock on the garage-level entry doors at the Watergate complex so that the team would be able to enter easily. Liddy regarded this as a reasonably discreet measure, as building maintenance people sometimes did the same to avoid having to fish for their keys. When team members arrived a few hours later, they noticed that the tape had been removed. They went ahead with the plan anyway, and McCord applied a new piece of tape over the lock. It was that second piece of tape that led a security guard to call the police, setting in motion the investigation that unraveled the operation and, eventually, the Nixon administration itself.

OOPS! SPECIAL SECTION: NOT-SO-GREAT WEAPONS OF WORLD WAR II

Nations fighting World War II rushed to come up with innovative weapons that would turn the tide of battle. Many of these weapons were not terribly well thought out.

A BATTY IDEA: PROJECT X-RAY

Shortly after declaring war on Japan, the United States looked for a way to attack the Japanese mainland. Somebody at the Pentagon had a flash of inspiration: Tiny incendiary bombs could be strapped to the chests of bats, and the bats could then be dropped over Japanese cities. When the bats landed, they would chew through the string that attached the bomb to their bodies, detonating it and setting fire to the closely packed, rickety wooden structures that made Japanese cities virtual tinderboxes.

The plan went forward under the code name "Project X-ray." A 1-ounce incendiary bomb was developed that would flare for 8 minutes with a 22-inch flame. Two million bats were drafted from caves in the Southwest. After nearly two years of development, the bat bombs were ready to be tested in New Mexico. Unfortunately, several of them escaped and set fires that destroyed a large aircraft hangar and a general's staff car. The army suspended all further work on the project.

The navy took over with a fresh approach: The bats would be frozen into hibernation for the bombing run so that there would be no danger that they would prematurely detonate. This plan was tested in August 1944 and revealed a crucial flaw. The chilled bats did not awaken after they were dropped out of the bombers, sleeping peacefully as they reached terminal velocity and augered into the ground. This would undoubtedly have disconcerted the Japanese, though probably not sufficiently to justify the effort. At this point it occurred to the top brass in the navy that it would be easier just to drop bombs and leave the bats in peace.

Over $2 million had been spent on Project X-ray when it was scrapped, and that doesn't include the cost of the hangar and the car.

TOO BIG FOR BATTLE: THE MAUS

In June 1942, with his army tied down on the Russian front, Hitler decided he needed an overwhelming new weapon to break the stalemate. To design it, he called upon Dr. Ferdinand Porsche, designer of the Volkswagen Beetle and, later, the sports cars. Code-named "Maus" (Mouse), it was to be the largest, most heavily armored tank ever seen, a kind of land battleship.

Porsche got to work, and by early 1944 had completed two working prototypes, 30 feet long and 20 feet high. Their armor at the front was 12 inches thick and averaged 9 1/2 inches elsewhere, making the tanks invulnerable to enemy fire. They had 1,500 horsepower diesel engines driving generators that powered motors in each of the tanks' hubs. Each Maus weighed 210 tons. Hitler's vision had been realized, but the Panzer Kampfwagen Maus II had certain obvious flaws that had not been discussed, since those who worked for Der Führer knew better than to question his judgment. When the Mouse was driven through villages, it smashed cobblestone streets and cracked the foundations of buildings. Its vibrations shattered windows. When it left the road, its enormous weight caused it to sink into the ground.

The project had to be dropped, and the two prototypes were destroyed at Kummersdorf in late 1944 before they could be captured by advancing Allied forces.

PAVLOVIAN DOGS: THE DOG MINE

The Russians came up with World War II's worst concept in anti-tank warfare, the dog mine. Dogs were fed underneath tanks, training them to associate the underside of a tank with their next meal. The plan was to strap bombs to their backs and then, after starving them for a day, release them as German tanks approached. When the dogs ran under the Panzers, a trigger on their backs would set off the bombs.

When Russian troops let loose the hounds of war they soon realized that they had overlooked one thing. Though the dogs had learned to associate tanks with food, the association was with Russian tanks. They performed their kamikaze mission against their masters, and many would say it served the Russians right.

An entire Russian division was forced to retreat as a consequence of the dog mines, and the operation was immediately canceled.

ANOTHER CLASSIC LINE FROM MAE WEST

Mae West was nothing if not a trouper when she starred as the ingenue in *Sextette* at age 86. When she arrived on the set, the crew tried to flatter her by complimenting her well-preserved appearance. "You don't look a day over twenty-nine!" one lied. "Thanks a lot," she retorted, "I'm *supposed* to be twenty-six."

Her infirmities necessitated some unusual measures. Due to her nearsightedness, her positions on the set had to be marked with sandbags. Because she had difficulty remembering her lines, a small radio receiver was built into her wig, and the director fed her her lines as needed. This caused some confusion on the set. For one thing, the other actors could hear the answers to lines they had not yet delivered, throwing them off. Worse was one occasion when Mae's receiver picked up a signal from a passing police helicopter. During a romantic scene the leading lady purred, "Traffic on the Hollywood Freeway is bogged down."

WHAM-O'S FAILED FAD

The Wham-O Corporation of San Gabriel, California, has had an extraordinary record with fads, bringing us the Hula Hoop, the Superball and the Frisbee. No one bats a thousand, though, and one of Wham-O's big ideas disappeared without a trace. The company took a quantity of mink remnants, punched out 2-inch donut shapes and covered the backs with stick-em. The concept? "Mink Stoles for the Belly Button."

Somehow American youth resisted the lure of this novel navel accessory.

WOODROW WILSON DID *WHAT*?

After Woodrow Wilson's first wife died, he started courting Edith Galt, a socially prominent Washington widow.

In 1915 the *Washington Post* mentioned in its society section that Wilson had taken Mrs. Galt to the theater. Trying to communicate to its readers the fact that the president had spent more time entertaining his date with conversation than paying attention to the performance, it wrote: "the President spent much of the evening entering Mrs. Galt."

THE END OF THE WORLD HAS BEEN POSTPONED

Every few years we hear about a prophet who convinces a group of followers that the world will end on a specific date. They sell their possessions and wait all night on some hilltop to rise into heaven. So far, at least, each such apocalyptic moment has ended with believers plodding dejectedly back down to rejoin the rest of us. One such misfire is usually enough to cast doubt on a prophet's prescience, but the nineteenth-century doomsayer William Miller made a career out of announcing Judgment Day, only to predict anew when the day came and went nonjudgmentally.

Miller was a fervent Baptist who studied the Bible through his own peculiar prism, which he called his "Rules of Interpretation." Like the Dylanologists of the 1960s who assumed that every Bob Dylan lyric had a secret, symbolic meaning, Miller believed that the Bible was a heavily encrypted text. "Mountains," for example, meant governments, and "days" stood for years. After studying the books of Daniel and Revelation, Miller arrived at the conclusion that the world would end on a date between March 21, 1843, and March 21, 1844. His sermons eloquently described the trumpets' clarion call, God's throne revealed through the parting of the clouds and the pitiful shrieks and howls of the souls consigned to damnation. Miller had many followers, and several newspapers supported his ministry, the largest being *Signs of the Times* and *The Midnight Cry*. During the fateful year numerous dates were proposed as The Big One, yet all proved duds. After the sun once again rose on March 22, 1844, Millerites began to be disrespectfully asked such questions as, "What! Not gone up yet? We thought you'd gone up! Wife didn't go up and leave you behind to burn, did she?"

Miller was undiscouraged, and his absolute conviction seemed to carry his flock along with him. He gave his calculations a thorough audit and reached a new conclusion—Judgment Day would absolutely, positively, have to be here no later than October 22, 1844.

Millerites grew frantic as the day approached. Merchants gave their inventory away, farmers left their crops to rot in the fields. Some went insane; there were murders and suicides. On the day itself some climbed hills or trees, positioning themselves to more easily leap into heaven at the proper moment. A Philadelphia man jumped the gun, leaping out of his third-story window while the law of gravity was still in effect. Some held umbrellas, laundry baskets and washtubs over their heads to facilitate rising. Even among the faithful, a group of society ladies waited apart, not wishing to ascend with the riffraff. One fashionable woman strapped herself to a trunk of clothes, so she could remain stylish in the afterlife.

October 23 dawned, another humdrum morning on Planet Earth, like billions before it and God-only-knows how many yet to come. The Millerites wandered away to pick up where they'd left off. Were they totally disgusted and disillusioned with William Miller and everything he'd told them? No, his movement still lives on in the form of several modern-day churches, the largest among them being the Seventh-Day Adventists, with a worldwide membership of over 3 million.

MASTERMINDS BEHIND THE WORLD TRADE CENTER BOMBING

When a terrorist bomb blew out the garage levels of the World Trade Center on February 26, 1993, the FBI warned the public not to expect a quick-and-easy solution to the crime. Of course, that was before the FBI realized that it was not dealing with criminal masterminds. A fragment of the van carrying the bomb carried a vehicle identification number, which quickly led investigators to a Ryder Truck rental outlet in Jersey City, New Jersey. The proprietor told them about one Mohammed Salameh, who had made rather a pest of himself trying to get back his $400 deposit on the van, claiming it had been stolen. Salameh had used his correct name, address and phone number when renting the vehicle, and his receipt was impregnated with traces of the explosives he had been handling. Two weeks after the bombing, on his fourth visit to the Ryder offices in search of his deposit, Salameh was arrested.

"He didn't have a clue," said Patrick Galasso, owner of the rental company. "He just wanted the money."

WRONG WAY CORRIGAN: A HERO IN SPITE OF HIMSELF

For the older generation, "Wrong Way Corrigan" was a catch-phrase used to describe someone who fouled up so badly it strained belief.

Douglas Corrigan was a pilot who took off from New York on July 16, 1938, headed for Los Angeles, and managed to wind up in Dublin, Ireland, instead. He claimed that his main compass had failed, and that in consulting his backup compass he had followed the wrong end of the needle, heading east instead of west as he flew above the cloud layer. "After 25 hours I decided to descend...The mountains didn't look like California...," he told reporters.

Many doubted Corrigan's tale, believing that he had intended to cross the ocean all along in emulation of his idol Charles Lindbergh. Corrigan denied this and successfully passed lie detector tests. He also had not prepared himself for a transatlantic flight, carrying no water and not enough food, no warm clothing and no maps of the Atlantic.

Corrigan became a folk hero and a fixture of the language by accidentally accomplishing what Lindbergh had only achieved through careful and determined effort.

JACKIE GLEASON LAYS EGG

The average TV viewer has suffered countless insults to his taste and intelligence, and does he ever get an apology? Well, he did get one once.

In 1960 Jackie Gleason, then under contract to CBS, went to the network with a proposal for a game show he would host called "You're in the Picture." The show would be based on the old Coney Island gag where customers poked their heads through holes in painted sets for comic photos. In Gleason's version, celebrity contestants would poke their heads through pictures they could not see, and would have to guess what the scene was by asking Gleason questions, to which he would respond with appropriate hints and wisecracks. The executives saw several problems with the format. There was no way for the stars to guess the answer until Gleason gave it to them, which eliminated any competition or suspense, and the audience couldn't play along as it would see the scene at the outset. Nevertheless, the network agreed to develop "You're in the Picture," afraid of upsetting the temperamental Gleason.

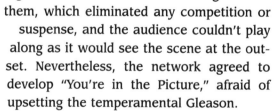

The show debuted on January 20, 1961, and was an absolute, unmitigated failure. The critics hated it and so did the public.

The next week, Gleason, The Great One, appeared alone on a bare stage and apologized to the American people for daring to insult them with such a rotten program. As he periodically drained and refilled a coffee cup with something he strongly hinted was not coffee, Gleason filled the half-hour with self-deprecation.

"We had a show last week that laid the biggest bomb. I've seen bombs in my day, but this made the H-bomb look like a two-inch salute." He had the stagehands haul out a piece of the scenery from the previous week's show and cracked, "Notice the stagehands have their backs to the audience. Even they don't want to be associated with this thing."

The TV audience loved this confessional, but the producers were aghast. By so trashing the show, Gleason had made it impossible to try to repair it, or to use the additional episode that had already been filmed. One of the show's sponsors was outraged that Gleason appeared drunk, and pulled its backing. Total losses from the apology amounted to a half million dollars at a time when that was considered real money.

ZAMBIAN SPACE PROGRAM STILL EARTHBOUND

During its coverage of Zambia's independence celebration in October 1964, *Time* magazine took note of the fledgling nation's nascent space program. The director of Zambia's "National Academy of Science, Space Research and Philosophy," Edward Mukuka Nkoloso, a grade school science teacher, pledged that his nation would beat the U.S. and the Soviet Union to the moon. Taking no time off for the independence festivities, Nkoloso was already actively training 12 prospective astronauts, including one 16-year-old girl. Most of the instruction involved 50-gallon oil drums, in which trainees were spun around at the end of a rope and rolled down hills in order to prepare them for the rigors of space flight. There was also extensive practice in learning to walk on their hands, which, according to Nkoloso, is "the only way humans can walk on the moon."

THE GOLDEN BANANA PEEL

Winner: Dan Quayle

Sorry to be so obvious, but we have to go where the evidence leads us. Quayle has a rare ability to take the most mundane declarative statement and mangle it into a syntactical disaster, in which any evidence of an underlying coherent thought is nowhere to be found. This attribute, while inconsequential in a high school gym teacher, is somewhat

*unnerving in the man who stood first in line for the presidency, a
responsibility he shouldered always with that strange, blank, deer-
in-the-headlights look on his face.*

Some retrospective highlights:

While visiting Hawaii, Dan Quayle issued the following analysis of Hawaii's special significance in America's Pacific strategy:
"Hawaii has always been a very pivotal role in the Pacific. It is
in the Pacific. It is a part of the United States that is an island
that is right here." Quayle also had something to say about
Hawaii's universal health care program: "Hawaii is a unique
state. It is a small state. It is a state that is by itself. It is a—it is
different than the other forty-nine states. Well, all states are different, but it's got a particularly unique situation."

Quayle was an outspoken believer that America needed to
maintain its investment in space exploration. His thoughts on
the significance of Mars were at least as coherent as his
thoughts on Hawaii: "Mars is essentially in the same orbit. Mars
is somewhat the same distance from the sun, which is very
important. We have seen pictures where there are canals, we
believe, and water. If there is water, there is oxygen. If oxygen,
that means we can breathe." (An aide insisted to reporters that
the vice president had not meant to suggest that there was
water on Mars or that humans could breathe there.)

In a press
conference,
Quayle raised the
possibility of life
on Mars.

Addressing a group in American Samoa, Quayle offered the following social analysis: "You all look like happy campers to me. Happy campers you are. Happy campers you have been. And, as far as I am concerned, happy campers you will always be."

Quayle described the Holocaust as "an obscene period in our nation's history...this century's history...We all lived in this century. I didn't live in this century."

Visiting San Francisco after the earthquake, Quayle observed that "the loss of life will be irreplaceable."

When Chief of Staff John Sununu was forced to leave the Bush White House, Quayle observed, "This isn't a man who is leaving with his head between his legs."

He asserted that Republicans "understand the importance of bondage between parent and child."

Speaking to the United Negro College Fund, Quayle had some thoughts on the organization's well-known slogan, "A mind is a terrible thing to waste." As he put it, "What a waste it is to lose one's mind—or not to have a mind. How true that is."

Quayle has a propensity for saying precisely the opposite (presumably) of what he means. Examples:

On David Duke's chances in the Louisiana senatorial race: "Unfortunately, the people of Louisiana are not racists."

Hailing the U.S. victory in the Gulf War: "It was a stirring victory for the forces of aggression."

On Central America, he said the U.S. "condones the violence in El Salvador." He also said the U.S. expects Salvadoran leaders "to work toward the elimination of human rights."

Responding to a question about his numerous gaffes, he said: "I stand by all the misstatements that I've made."

In 1991 the Quayles sent out hundreds of custom-printed Christmas cards that contained a spelling error. It read: "May our nation continue to be the beakon [sic] of hope to the world."

Douglas McGrath, a columnist for *The Nation*, made up this quote and attributed it to Quayle: "The Civil War was the best war we've ever had because when you're fighting with yourself you're always going to win."

DRUGS AND TRAFFICKING

What amazed McGrath was that a number of people, including journalists, assumed that the quote was authentic. But then, why shouldn't they?

Perhaps the final blow to Quayle's credibility came during the presidential campaign of 1992. While looking in on a spelling bee at the Luis Munoz Rivera School in Trenton, New Jersey, Vice President Dan Quayle made a helpful suggestion to 12-year-old William Figueroa. The boy had correctly spelled the word "potato" on the blackboard, but Quayle, misguided by an incorrectly spelled flash card he'd been given, prompted him to add an "e" at the end.

Quayle's spelling mistake seemed to add an exclamation point to public perceptions of his bumbling persona. News commentators and late-night comedians took an unseemly delight in the gaffe. Figueroa felt badly for the veep. "I knew he was wrong. He probably feels embarrassed about that, probably mad a little...but I hope he can take it."

Quayle is not as dumb as everyone thinks he is—it wouldn't be possible. In fact, many close observers rate him higher in intelligence and political acumen than the president he served under. Even his detractors now grant that he was right about the social cost of single motherhood, and his criticism of the legal profession was well founded. Lastly, in Quayle's defense, it should be noted that an ABC News-*Washington Post* poll indicated that nearly a third of all voters admitted that they could not spell "potato," and an additional 4% said they did not know or had no opinion.

Still, for all he's said and done, a Golden Banana Peel to J. Danforth Quayle.

BIBLIOGRAPHY

Much of the information in this collection came from newspapers and periodicals, including the *New York Times, Washington Post, Christian Science Monitor, Wall Street Journal, New Haven Register, The Economist, Esquire* (especially its annual Dubious Achievement Awards), *Forbes, Time, Newsweek, National Geographic, The Progressive, Readers' Digest* and *Soldier of Fortune.*

Baldick, Robert. *The Duel.* Clarkson N. Potter, Inc.: New York, 1965

Cherry-Garrard, Apsley. *The Worst Journey in the World.* The Dial Press: New York, 1930

Christopher, Milbourne. *Houdini: The Untold Story.* Thomas Y. Crowell Company: New York, 1969

Cohen, Daniel. *Great Mistakes.* M. Evans and Co: New York, 1979

Coleman, Ray. *The Man Who Made the Beatles.* McGraw-Hill Publishing Company: New York, 1989

Collier, Peter and Horowitz, David. *The Fords: An American Epic.* Simon & Schuster: New York, 1987

Cooper, Robert. *Foibles, Follies and Foolish Deeds.* Signet: New York, 1993

Edwardes, Michael. *British India.* Taplinger Publishing Company: New York, 1968

Encyclopaedia Britannica, Inc. *Encyclopaedia Britannica.* Chicago, 1987

Felton, Bruce and Fowler, Mark. *The Best, Worst, and Most Unusual.* Galahad Books: New York, 1994

Generous, Kevin M. *Vietnam: The Secret War.* Gallery Books: New York, 1985

Gilbert, James. *The World's Worst Aircraft.* St. Martin's Press: New York, 1975

Givens, Bill. *Film Flubs.* Carol Publishing Group: New York, 1990

Givens, Bill. *Film Flubs: The Sequel.* Carol Publishing Group: New York, 1992

Goldberg, M. Hirsh. *The Book of Lies.* William Morrow and Company, Inc.: New York, 1990

Goldberg, M. Hirsh. *The Complete Book of Greed.* William Morrow and Company, Inc.: New York, 1994

Gordon, Dr. Richard. *Great Medical Disasters.* Stein and Day: New York, 1983

Henry, William A. *The Great One: The Life and Legend of Jackie Gleason.* Doubleday: New York, 1992

Hume, Ivor Nöel. *The Virginia Adventure.* Alfred A. Knopf: New York, 1994

Kemp, Anthony. *The Maginot Line: Myth and Reality.* Stein & Day: New York, 1982

Keyes, Ralph. *"Nice Guys Finish Seventh": False Phrases, Spurious Sayings, and Familiar Misquotations.* HarperCollins Publishers, Inc.: New York, 1992

Kohut, John J. and Sweet, Roland. *Countdown to the Millenium.*

Penguin Books: New York, 1992

Kohut, John J., and Sweet, Roland. *News From the Fringe*. Penguin Books: New York, 1993

Kohut, John J. *Stupid Government Tricks*. Penguin Books: New York, 1995

Kramer, Michael; Roberts, Sam. *"I Never Wanted To Be Vice-President of Anything!" An Investigative Biography of Nelson Rockefeller*. Basic Books, Inc.: New York, 1976

Liddy, G. Gordon. *Will*. St. Martin's Press: New York, 1980

Louis, David. 2201 *Fascinating Facts*. Crown Publishers: New York, 1983

MacKay, Charles. *Extraordinary Popular Delusions and the Madness of Crowds*. Barnes & Noble Books: New York, 1993

Marsano, William A. *Man Suffocated By Potatoes: Intelligence Reports from Planet Earth*. New American Library: New York, 1987

Medved, Harry and Michael. *The Hollywood Hall of Shame*. The Putnam Publishing Group: New York, 1984

Morgan, Chris and Langford, David. *Facts and Fallacies: A Book of Definitive Mistakes and Misguided Predictions*. Webb & Bower Limited: Devon, England, 1981

Morris, Scot. *The Book of Strange Facts and Useless Information*. Doubleday & Company: Garden City, New York, 1979

Mosely, Leonard. *Lindbergh: A Biography*. Doubleday & Company: New York, 1976

Nash, Bruce and Zullo, Allan. *The Misfortune 500*. Pocket Books: New York, 1988

Nash, Bruce and Zullo, Allan. *The Sports Hall of Shame*. Pocket Books: New York, 1987

Octopus Books Limited. *That's Life*. Treasure Press: London, 1989

Onoda, Hiroo. *No Surrender: My Thirty-Year War*. Harper & Row, Publishers, Inc.: New York, 1974

Paggie, Michael J. *Some Days Nothing Goes Right*. Barnes & Noble: New York, 1993

Panati, Charles. *Panati's Extraordinary Endings of Practically Everything and Everybody*. Harper & Row: New York, 1989

Phelan, James. *Howard Hughes: The Hidden Years*. Random House, Inc.: New York, 1976

Pile, Stephen. *The Incomplete Book of Failures*. E.P. Dutton: New York, 1979

Pile, Stephen. *Cannibals in the Cafeteria*. Harper & Row, Publishers: New York, 1988

Poundstone, William. *Big Secrets*. William Morrow & Company, Inc.: New York, 1983

Pringle, Laurence. *The Earth Is Flat—and Other Great Mistakes*. William Morrow and Company: New York, 1983

Ross, Walter S. *The Last Hero: Charles A. Lindbergh*. Harper & Row: New York, 1964

Shenkman, Richard; Rieger, Kurt. *One-Night Stands with American History*. Quill Press, 1980

Sheperd, Chuck; Kohut, John J.; and Sweet, Roland. *News of the Weird.* Penguin Books: New York, 1989

Sheperd, Chuck; Kohut, John J.; and Sweet, Roland. *More News of the Weird.* Penguin Books: New York, 1990

Steinberg, Neil. *Complete and Utter Failure.* Doubleday: New York, 1994

Tamarkin, Bob. *Rumor Has It.* Prentice Hall General Reference: New York, 1993

Time-Life. *The Seafarers Series. The Pirates.* Time-Life Books: New York, 1978

Time-Life. *The Seafarers Series. The Pacific Navigators.* Time-Life Books: New York, 1980

Train, John. *True Remarkable Occurrences.* Clarkson N. Potter, Inc., Publishers: New York, 1978

Train, John. *Most Remarkable Occurrences.* HarperCollins: New York, 1990

Wallace, Irving; Wallechinsky, David; Wallace, Amy. *Significa.* E. P. Dutton, Inc.: New York, 1983

Wallechinsky, David; Wallace, Amy; Wallace, Irving. *The Book of Predictions.* William Morrow and Company, Inc.: New York, 1980.

Welsh, Douglas. *The History of the Vietnam War.* Exeter Books: New York, 1986

Yenne, Bill. *The World's Worst Aircraft.* Dorset Press: Greenwich, CT, 1993

INDEX

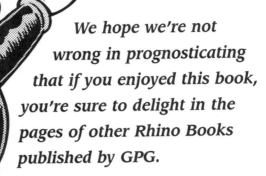

We hope we're not wrong in prognosticating that if you enjoyed this book, you're sure to delight in the pages of other Rhino Books published by GPG.

Forgotten Fads and Fabulous Flops

This book's author, Paul Kirchner's previous book that *Boomer* magazine critiqued as "a wonderful, heavily illustrated bundle of fun." A re-introduction to famous American can't misses: the Edsel, the Susan B. Anthony dollar and 3-D movies, as well as more unbelievable and esoteric rages that just didn't last. Remember Goldfish Swallowing, the Drinking Man's Diet and the Topless Swimsuit?

The Best of the World's Worst

The world's worst army, the world's worst state to live in, the world's worst animal sex maniacs...it's all here in this 192 page collection compiled by Marvel's Stan Lee. *The National Enquirer* described it as "Hilarious blunders and side-splitting stories."

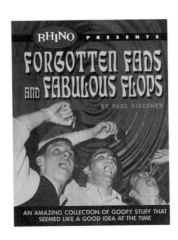

Va Va Voom!

The first truly comprehensive account of the breathtaking glamour girls from the 1940s and '50s—pioneers such as Mamie Van Doren, Lili St. Cyr, June Wilkinson, Stella Stevens, Blaze Starr, Candy Barr and others, as well as icons Monroe, Mansfield and Bardot—compellingly told in their own words, and jammed with photographs.

Everything You Know Is Wrong

Many people suspect that TV and the movies misinform us with unscrupulous frequency, but history books don't get it wrong too, do they? We know Cleopatra was Egyptian, Columbus proved the world was round, and Napoleon was short, right? Wrong! What about the stuff everybody knows? We have five senses, you only use 10% of your brain, and carrots are good for your eyes, right? WRONG! Get the low-down on these and hundreds of other lies, myths and misconceptions in Rhino Books' *Everything you Know Is Wrong*, the book that dares to ask, HOW DO YOU KNOW WHAT YOU KNOW IS RIGHT?!

If your local bookstore is too unhip to have these treasures continually in stock, call Rhino's mail order department at 1-800-432-0020. While you're at it, have the customer service rep send you Rhino's latest comprehensive catalogue if you're interested in checking out what *Spin* magazine and others have called "America's Best Record Label" has to offer. Toot! Toot!